Sacred Times

Sacred Times

A New Approach to Festivals

WILLIAM BLOOM

Findhorn Press

Set in Benguiat and Garamond Bold on Mackintosh SE.
Design and layout by Philip Mielewczyk; cover design by
Claudia Klingemann, Bay Area Graphics.
Printed and bound by Billings & Sons, Worcester, England.

Printed on recycled paper

For Sabrina

Acknowledgements

This book was originally going to be two booklets: one on the Solstices, Equinoxes, Fire Festivals and lunar cycle; and the other on the human cycle of birth, marriage and death. But Sandra Kramer of the Findhorn Press and a meditation in the Universal Sanctuary at the Findhorn Foundation persuaded me to combine them into one volume. It has been a real pleasure doing this work and I am grateful for the inspiration to present it in this form.

I need also to thank the hospitality of Hinko and Marika Ziglic and the Yugoslav island of Serakane, where most of this was written. My deep gratitude also to Marika Pogacnik, Marko Pogacnik and Sabrina Dearborn who provided an extraordinary ambience in which to work. The final editing was done at the Meitheal Community in north-west Ireland.

Some of the information in this book previously appeared in a very abbreviated form on the poster *Celebrating the Year—The Annual Cycle of Spiritual Festivals* (Findhorn Press) and in my book *Meditation in a Changing World* (Gothic Image).

Contents

Introduction

The purpose of this short book is to stimulate the reader into an active involvement with spiritual festivals—festivals of the human life cycle and festivals of Gaia and the cosmos. It may be that the reader will positively dislike my ideas about how to approach these events. It may also be that the reader will think that I have ignored crucial moments, elements and approaches and overemphasised unimportant features.

A further criticism that might rightly be levelled is the cheek of the book's brevity. The subject matter deserves deep consideration and not just 120 well-spaced pages; each topic within it deserves a book to itself and more careful attention.

All of these criticisms may be true and, in particular, I apologise for the brevity. My purpose, however, is to stimulate. I will feel as if I have done something worthwhile if people, having read *Sacred Times* and even disagreeing with its approach, are drawn nevertheless into contemplating the significance of the festivals and, from that contemplation, find that they want actively to research, work with and co-create them.

I do not want to tell anybody what to do, but I do think these festivals and a sacred approach to them are important. All time, all space and all events are sacred, but certain convergences are 'power points' in space and time. To ignore them is to ignore our spiritual environment and spiritual ecology.

So here, in this short book, is an introduction and a possible approach to them. The whole field is extraordinarily rich and beautiful, stretching our imagination and consciousness. I feel privileged to be involved in helping your relationship with these festivals unfold.

Part One
Preparation

1
Opening Thoughts

The Celebrant Within

When people used to ask me, as a child, what I wanted to be when I grew up, I always gave a definite answer. But, in truth, like most of us, I was not certain. In my early teens, however, I had a minor revelation when a friend asked me the same question and I heard myself answer, "What I really want is to be able to choose each day who I am and what I do." In many ways I still feel the same today.

When I first gave that answer, I spent time thinking about the various possibilities and one of the roles I considered was that of priest. But I wanted to be a priest who belonged either to no religion or to all religions. This was an easy thought for me because I instinctively had little—if any—respect for religious organisations or churches. The greater the religious organisation, the more distant it seemed from the essence of its founding inspiration. Because of this, the idea of ordination—that an organisation or bureaucracy could decree someone a priest—rang hollow. People knew in their hearts if they were priests: this was the true priesthood.

Alongside this instinctive caution about organised religion, I also had my own spiritual perspective. From a very early age I had had an ongoing mystical experience in relation to the great blue dome of the sky above us. The blue dome fascinated, inspired and brought me an experience near bliss. The sky for me was the roof of a great and wonderful temple. We all existed within this temple. Buildings, even great cathedrals or pyramids, were but a pale reflection of this *real* temple and we—all humans, all life—were sacred beings within it. If we were to pray, I thought, let us drop on our knees in awe within the true temple. Let us fall on our knees in the street, in a field, anywhere. We needed no man-made churches.

In short I had little respect for the religious institutions and priestly hierarchies, but a wondering devotion to the greater sacred reality.

Of course, I am not the only one with such feelings, thoughts and inspirations. Many of us, in one form or another, have the same spiritual experiences, but there is a sad tendency amongst us to forget them, as our society does not teach us to honour them. But these experiences and perceptions live on in our hearts and in our subconscious—and they reawaken.

New Ways and a New Authenticity

We are in changing times. Our culture and technology are continuously transforming, and the intellectual certainties of the last few hundred years are no longer secure. The revelations of sub-atomic physics and modern psychology have fatally wounded fixed ideas concerning rationality and the nature of existence. The new scientific insights are showing us a multi-dimensional universe, a universe that we want to explore. But how can we explore it? Scientific instruments are not sensitive enough to do anything but hint at these realities.

And as these new sciences point towards this multi-dimensional reality, we are also experiencing a profound intuitive desire to begin a re-exploration of spiritual realities. This urge to explore inner realities, then, is both rational and intuitive. And in this new exploration people are prepared to use any tools or belief systems that might help. Ideas from the past are reappearing as people examine all the different traditions of sacred wisdom. All kinds of breathing, yoga and psychological techniques are being tried that bring the practitioner into an altered state of consciousness. In fact almost any idea or technique seems

2

worth looking at once, just to see if it holds a seed of enlightenment. We cannot use scientific instruments, so we must, therefore, rely on the greatest of the human tools: our consciousness.

There is, though, another theme in the midst of all this. It is our need to find a new *authenticity* in our spiritual lives. We wish to resurrect—to bring back fully into our consciousness—the sacred dimension of life, but we want to do this in a way that honours personal freedom and personal growth. In essence, then, we are turning to the teachings and experiences of what is called the ageless wisdom, but we are doing so with completely new attitudes.

One of these attitudes, which I believe is central for all of us, is that we will not yield spiritual authority to anyone or any idea unless we are absolutely certain in our hearts and minds that it is right to do so.

To many of us it seems that we are surrounded by people who are still subservient to spiritual authority, *simply* because of social and psychological constraints. There seems to be no inner inspiration in their choice of beliefs. Their religion comes from outside rather than from within, bringing social identity and psychological security rather than spiritual inspiration. The words of Rousseau have not been bettered: "Man is born free, and everywhere he is in chains." And, as he wrote elsewhere: "Everything is good when it leaves the Creator's hands; everything degenerates in the hands of man."

One of the key features of the currently emerging culture is this ongoing inner battle to free ourselves from the hooks and delusions of social-psychological reality and to come to a true understanding of our identity. If there is a common dedication, it is to find an authentic spiritual experience of who we are, why we are and where we are—and to have a sense of its truthfulness from a private source within rather than a so-called 'spiritual' authority out there.

This small book, then, has two purposes, both of them

3

entwined and neither stronger than the other. One is to present the essence of the major spiritual festivals so that we can be more deeply attuned to and understanding of them. The other is to empower us to become our own sacred celebrants.

Religions are Always Changing and They Need To

A key element of our changing culture is that we are discarding old religious forms and re-creating our spiritual and sacred world. We are like a wise serpent, shedding an old skin behind us.

Yet the current emergence and creation of a new culture is not an easy process. It feels as if everything is being created anew. At the same time we know that we are working with dimensions which always have been and which always shall be. Our emerging culture is a reinterpretation of eternal realities and it is also a response to new spiritual impulses. In fact there is always this beautiful contradiction: that the eternal spiritual dimension is itself always in the process of change. It is caught in the reality of its own process, its inherent dynamic always unfolding to become more itself, more love, more its essence—and we, in turn, are always interpreting this essence, creating new cultural and religious forms and new methods of opening to spirit.

Thus, every age and culture has its appropriate religious forms and inspirations. They come and they go. Religions and belief systems are not fixed objects to be perpetually venerated. To think that any religious structure is perpetual is to misunderstand the dynamism of spiritual revelation. For this reason alone, it is fair to say that much religious form, as we have known it over the last one, two or three thousand years, is simply out of date or becoming out of date. Also—and here is a real tragedy—in many ways the major religions and their religious festivals have become greatly distanced from the essence and intentions of their spiritual founders.

Furthermore, and worse, the major religions and their festivities are responsible for great and sometimes terrible divisiveness. These religious forms more often than not actively exclude people from other faiths. The religious structures, churches and priestly hierarchies feed this divisiveness and exclusivity; and any talk of unity, ecumenicalism or synthesis is spoken of only from within the psychological walls of the particular religious system. We cannot allow this to continue. It is too destructive, too hypocritical, too disempowering of humanity's natural spiritual rights. Many of us, therefore, seek actively to change this corrupt system. There are many different religions, mystical flowers, each with the potential to blossom perfectly, but now growing like unwanted weeds choking our garden.

Many of us also believe that certain religious *attitudes* are out of date as well. One of these attitudes, which now seems completely inappropriate, is a devotion to form, continuity and stability. There is nothing wrong with form, continuity or stability in themselves. What is questionable is a *devotion* to them. There needs to be a greater understanding of the Aquarian principle that everything is in the process of fluid change. *Each breath, new patterns.*

In working with these festivals, then, we need to honour the fact that new forms are emerging. We need to experiment. We need to be open. And having found something that works for us, we need still to remain open. Good ceremony, good festivity, has a quality of fluid changing dance, not rigidity.

There is the ever-sobering thought that what we attune to today as being perfect will inevitably one day be redundant. So, no matter how certain I may seem about how these things are or ought to be, I attempt as best I can always to be open to change. In essence we stay aligned with love and grace, but the form and shape of their manifestation are always changing.

The Beauty of the Emerging Festivals

The beauty of a cycle of festivals based on the natural rhythm of the Sun and the Moon is that their foundation is not in human religious ideology, even if of the most exquisite kind, but in ecological realities. Whoever you are, wherever you live upon this planet, whatever your culture or faith, the rhythms of the Sun, the seasons and the Moon exist. Therefore to take these as the signal and inspiration for spiritual festivals is to be attuned in an ecologically harmonious way, one that works with our earthly and cosmic spiritual environment.

I love the natural cycle of spiritual festivals because their timing and their essence are free of human ideology and theology. If we were to remove humanity from Earth, the Solstices, Equinoxes, lunar rhythm and Fire festivals would still remain. When we celebrate and work with these events we are falling into an ecological pattern that already exists. We are working with a natural rhythm that brings us into greater harmony with the Earth and with the cosmos. We are not celebrating any one religious teacher's ideas, thereby cutting ourselves off from those who do not share the same belief. The full Moon is the full Moon is the full Moon, wherever and whoever you are. The Solstice tells a cosmic story to Christians, Moslems, Jews, Hindus and Buddhists alike.

I love these festivals, therefore, because they hold the promise of a world without religious conflict. In a way, they are the inner essence and rhythm of the Green movement. We have all been learning about our environmental responsibilities because of our ecological relationships. But what about inner ecology? What about cosmic ecology? Attunement to and working with these festivals can bring us into a joyful celebration of the great inner ecological relationships.

As we become increasingly aware of our environment, as we become increasingly sensitive to spiritual and inner dimensions, it makes sense that our spiritual festivals be signalled by and interwoven with the natural rhythms of our cosmos.

Over the last century a new awareness of these natural festivals has been steadily growing. An increasing number of people have been adjusting the quality and nature of their individual and group meditations according to the lunar cycle. Equally, many have been celebrating life and creation in rhythm with the Solstices, Equinoxes and Fire festivals. My intention is to clarify these new strands and to present the beginnings of a coherent picture. Spiritual work with the lunar rhythm in particular has been described in detail by the great Tibetan teacher Djwahl Kuhl, with his secretary Alice Bailey, and many groups over several decades have been working with full Moon meditations. There is, therefore, a certain degree of clarity about how to work with the lunar rhythm.

This clarity, however, does not exist to such a great degree for the Equinoxes, Solstices and Fire festivals. There is much historical and anthropological information as to how these festivals were celebrated in the past, but how they are to be celebrated in our culture and in the future is only now emerging. In particular, groups associated with the revival of the Celtic tradition and involved in what are called Earth Mysteries are showing the way forward. It is possible, however, to investigate the essential inspiration of these festivals and, in understanding their inspiration, we come closer to seeing how we can work with and experience them.

All this has great relevance for the future of religion, for I believe that the great thought structures and organisations of the contemporary world religions will melt away. Men and women will seek truth within and use any mode or path that seems appropriate, but they will come together for these natural celebrations. The Solstices and Equinoxes will honour our cosmic relationships; the Fire festivals will celebrate our relationship with the angelic realms; and the lunar cycle will be used for intense inner work and spiritual service.

I love these festivals also for the spiritual strength they give us. It is beautiful to see men and women, ordained by nothing other than their own inner calling, leading ceremonies, meditations and festivals. The beauty of sacred celebration and the beauty of leading sacred celebration is that if we get our attitude and atmosphere right, then we can act and talk in full alignment with our inner selves and spirit. In spiritual ceremony our inner life becomes externalised into three-dimensional earthly life and the two realities can integrate.

My hope, then, is that the ceremonies in this book act as an inspiration for people to take on their own spiritual roles. Working with sacred ritual can be a deeply empowering experience and I advise people not to be cowardly about their own spiritual authority. Carefully accepting this authority can introduce us to an empowering and compassionate spiritual dignity. I can think of many friends who, despite nervousness and serious misgivings, have nevertheless led sacred celebrations and found the experience transformative.

Why We Festival Together

We possess, I believe, profound spiritual instincts for coming together in sacred gatherings in order to celebrate and to be of religious service. These are instincts very different from those that give comfort and euphoria in a crowd or mob. It is worth examining, then, why we should want to come together in spiritual festivals in the first place. It seems to me that there are various distinct aspects which work separately and together. These aspects are concerned with: *Psychological Well-Being, Ecological Harmony, Spiritual Inspiration* and *Spiritual Service.* Let us look at each of them in turn.

Psychological Well-Being

It is obvious that we humans gather together because we like each other's company and because it brings us positive psychological benefits of one kind or another. Some of these benefits can be quite crude, but others have a deeper dynamic.

Human incarnation and the path of psychological and spiritual growth are not easy. The very nature of being human carries paradox and poignancy. There are two major paradoxes. Our inner source holds a note of unity, yet our incarnate experience is of separation. Our inner source holds a note of perfection, yet our incarnate experience is of imperfection. *We are one, yet separate. We are perfect, yet imperfect.*

As a species we are strung out by these dualities and we all of us suffer anxiety and insecurity.

When we gather together, then, with our fellow creatures to acknowledge sacred realities—in whatever form—we bring a creature comfort to each other. From that same place in our bodies that hugs a tree and cradles an infant, we radiate a magnetic comfort. This gives us psychological security and encouragement. Some people find this experience embarrassing or sentimental. If we are self-aware and recognise it for what it is, it is to be valued. The nurture of these situations can soothe our insecurity and anxiety, and strengthen us.

There is also enormous comfort to be gained from watching fellow members of our species acting in a sacred way. Suddenly our private awareness of spiritual realities becomes a shared public reality and, with this experience, we change our whole perception of society. Instead of seeing it as made up of savage and competitive humans, we recognise that it consists of fellow creatures of spirit, sharing the same difficulties and challenges and the same spiritual purpose.

Ecological Harmony

There is also the ecological dimension. As a species we are beginning to learn once again how to respect and honour our environment, but we have as yet focused only on the tip of the iceberg. Our awareness of the three-dimensional ecology around us is just the start of a far greater and more expansive awareness. Our true ecological environment is both a visible and an invisible one. It is also not only local and planetary, but cosmic. We live, in fact, in a world of multi-dimensional energies and relationships. In spiritual festivals we not only acknowledge these relationships, but we also celebrate them, honouring our interdependence with the many different life forces, beings, dimensions and consciousnesses.

Later in this book I shall go into these relationships in greater detail, but for the moment let us just list them briefly. They are: all our fellow creatures who share our space on Gaia and in the cosmos; time itself and the seasons; the Sun, the Moon, the constellations of the zodiac, the greater universe; the angelic, fairy and devic realms.

In our spiritual festivals we pause and give time and gratitude to these relationships, some obvious and visible, some discreet and invisible—mostly ignored—and profoundly deserving of our attention.

Spiritual Inspiration

Movement along the path of spiritual change and growth is not a smooth ride. We have our times of intense enlightenment and illumination, but we also have our lengthy times of inertia and depression. It is as if the gods and goddesses throw us morsels of spiritual experience and insight: "This is what it feels like. Now you do it!"

Our souls set up experiences for us of what it will be like at our next stage of growth. We have a new experience of love or grace; our meditation suddenly takes us into a new form or peak of consciousness. And then . . . ? Well, then we find ourselves back where we ever were and the real personal spiritual work begins. The task then is to find and adopt a spiritual practice that takes us *permanently* into that new state of consciousness. What was tasted by us, thrown to us by our souls or by godlings, must now become totally a part of us. Full repossession of that new consciousness may come gracefully and easily; but more often than not it will come only after sustained spiritual discipline, sometimes over many years.

The process is not easy and we may be tempted to give up. But if we give up, there will be a terrible cost in loss of self-respect and in a deep sense of spiritual bereavement—perhaps not conscious, but certainly simmering beneath the surface, frequently creating feelings of inferiority which are then compensated for by a personality ego inflation and sometimes spiritual pride.

The spiritual festivals can work fantastically upon us, both inspiring us with new experiences and providing us with an ongoing and rhythmic spiritual practice.

When groups do spiritual work together at the time of a festival, the group inner activity creates an energy field far greater than that which can be summoned up by an individual upon her or his own. Frequently, therefore, at the spiritual festivals we have heightened spiritual experiences. Instead of just letting the godlings throw those morsels of inspiration at us, we create the inspirations and peak experiences ourselves.

More than that, festivals can create a model, an archetypal scenario of humanity harmoniously at work together. In a magnetic and radiant way, this work then radiates outwards—in patterns and harmonics—to inspire others.

Spiritual Service, Channelling Energy
It is clear how working with the festivals is of spiritual service: we create inspiration and comfort; we honour the whole range of life forms, realities and dimensions which

intertwine with and affect our lives. But the festivals also work in other ways, invoking, creating and distributing healing energy, joy, enlightenment and love. At the festivals we become active participants interceding between heaven and earth, a column or maypole of energy linking spiritual and material dimensions.

Every human body and psyche possesses the natural gift of being able to function like a radio and like a broadcasting system. In the same way that a radio dial can be turned to tune into different wavelengths, so we can also tune ourselves into different wavelengths. And, like a radio, we can then turn up the volume and radiate them.

At festivals, as individuals and as groups, we place ourselves in resonance with 'high' good vibrations and we then channel and radiate them. Their radiation enters the vehicle and the psyche of Gaia and of humanity as a whole, helping and speeding spiritual unfoldment, empowering and healing.

Basic New Age Ideas

Some readers may come to this book with no knowledge of the basic ideas which underpin these ceremonies. It is helpful to understand them as they create the context and are the inspiration for the ceremonies. What follows, then, is a list of them. They are not meant to be a box of beliefs—get in and stay in. They are meant as an open-ended scaffolding on to which we can hang our experiences, wisdom and intuition. I produced this list in the Spring of 1989 and circulated it for criticism. I have made a few changes, but the major criticism was that the list did not catch the excitement and inspiration of our times. So, with the caution that the list is a dull representation of extraordinary realities, I hesitantly present it:

• All life—all existence—is the manifestation of Spirit, of the Unknowable, of that supreme consciousness known

12

by many different names in many different cultures.
• The purpose and dynamic of all existence is to bring love, wisdom, enlightenment . . . into full manifestation.
• All religions are the expression of this same inner reality.

• All life, as we perceive it with the five human senses or with scientific instruments, is only the outer veil of an invisible, inner and causal reality.
• Similarly, human beings are twofold creatures—with:
  i. an outer temporary personality
  and
  ii. a multi-dimensional inner being (soul or higher self).
• The outer personality is limited and tends towards materialism.
• The inner being is infinite and tends towards love.
• The purpose of the incarnation of the inner being is to bring the vibrations of the outer personality into a resonance of love.

• All souls in incarnation are free to choose their own spiritual path.

• Our true spiritual teachers are those souls who are liberated from the need to incarnate and who express unconditional love, wisdom and enlightenment. Some of these great beings are well-known and have inspired the world religions. Some are unknown and work invisibly.

• All life, in all its different forms and states, is interconnected energy—and this includes our deeds, feelings and thoughts. We, therefore, work with Spirit and these energies in co-creating our reality.
• Although held in the overall dynamic of cosmic love, we are jointly responsible for the state of our selves, of our environment and of all life.

• During this period of time, the evolution of the planet and of humanity has reached a point when we are undergoing a fundamental spiritual change in our individual and mass consciousness. This is why we talk of a New Age. This new consciousness is the result of the increasingly successful incarnation of what some people call the energies of cosmic love. This new consciousness demonstrates itself in an instinctive understanding of the sacredness and, in particular, the interconnectedness of all existence.

• This new consciousness and this new understanding of the dynamic interdependence of all life mean that we are currently in the process of evolving a completely new planetary culture.

In direct relation to the ceremonies for birth, marriage and death:

• *Birth* is understood as a soul taking on physical form in order to learn and to work with the process of manifesting perfect love and enlightenment.

• *Marriage* is understood as two people recognising that in committing themselves to being husband and wife they are choosing to accelerate their spiritual growth by working together to manifest perfect love and enlightenment.

• And *death* is understood as the soul having completed this cycle of learning and having chosen to return to an inner world of pure contemplation before, once again, seeking incarnate life.

14

2
Preparation
& Cleansing

Parting the Veils

Traditionally no ceremony is ever performed without special preparation and this preparation concerns the location and the participants. Why should this be so?

The whole purpose of ceremony is to bring spiritual awareness and a sacred atmosphere into the events and happenings of everyday life. A child is born, the Moon is full, a couple marries, the night is at its longest, or a friend dies. These are all common events, but they also have a profound inner significance. Because we are human and forgetful, it is easy for us to lose sight of the essence of these happenings. In ceremonies we create three-dimensional here-and-now sacred situations in which we cannot miss the spiritual significance of the events. But this spiritual perspective is not simply philosophical; it has also to do with real energies. In a sacred ceremony, the everyday three-dimensional world becomes infused with spiritual energy and atmospheres. The effective sacred ritual works to thin and dissolve the veil between the two realities.

When a sacred event is happening we can feel the change in atmosphere. Spirit enters tangibly into our space. In the Jewish kabbalistic tradition, this change of atmosphere is explained as being due to the presence of a multi-dimensional being or form of consciousness who is called the Shekinah. The Shekinah is female and graces sacred events with her presence, but she only does so in the presence of purity. She is also Grace.

A pure atmosphere, a cleansed location, a participant

who has prepared carefully—all these create the clean and open vibrations which allow sacred energies to enter into a situation. Perform a ceremony without preparation and in a dirty location, and the event will be a mess. We need to prepare ourselves and the location.

Personal Preparation

We live in a culture in which we have, over the last decades, thrown off the straightjacket of meaningless discipline. In particular we have been freeing ourselves from the disciplines and constrictions of a Piscean patriarchal culture in which we have obeyed certain rules and figures simply because we were expected to. Nowadays we choose our own rules and the people to whom we may temporarily surrender our authority. For many people the very concept of *discipline* sends a shudder down the spine. I, too, instinctively distrust any discipline to do with outside figures or ideas. But I honour self-discipline. I honour its rhythm, groundedness and clarity. Without it, spiritual practice would collapse. I watch my friends who have it and the centre and the clarity that it gives them.

We need to re-own spiritual self-discipline—spiritual effort. It is the most basic human tool that we have for our spiritual growth. And we need it if we are to act with integrity in ceremony. The body, the personality and the psyche of the celebrant need, according to the ancient metaphor, to form a pure temple for the work that is to be done. Sacred work, done in ceremony and for the sake of other people, has to be done with spiritual clarity.

It does not feel appropriate for me to go into detail as to how people should cleanse and prepare themselves. Each individual, in her silence, in her heart, in her inner being, knows what elements are required for spiritual focus. They have always been the same: daily silence, lowering the intake of food for a while and contemplation of inner truths. It is for each of us to prepare in the way that best suits us.

16

I would only add that it is not useful to become too intense. Fasting is helpful, but not if it causes you to pass out in the middle of a ceremony. Intense meditation is also wonderful, but not if you can no longer locate yourself in time and space. We need well-rounded, warm and anchored human beings in ceremony. Spaced-out ascetics are not the greatest ritualists.

In sacred celebration we need to be attuned to the highest and, at the same time, anchored in the here and now. Part of our preparation is to make certain that we really understand and are attuned to the ceremony and its words. There is no point in doing a ceremony unless we believe the words we are saying and communicate their significance. When the words are spoken, we need to hold a clear inner focus which is perfectly in tune with the intention of the ceremony. This means we have to understand the essence of the words and, almost without exception, this will require periods of study and contemplation before celebration.

If in doubt about your voice and style, practise aloud, alone and with friends, and be open to criticism and suggestions. Taking a voice workshop can also be useful. Of all things avoid pomposity and pretension. As you perform the ceremony, your body needs to be calm and relaxed. At your best, a ceremony is a walking meditation with the inner grace and rhythm of a sacred dance.

Ceremonies have to be conducted with a meditative attitude, otherwise it is impossible for the celebrant effectively to take responsibility for the atmosphere. If we are leading ceremonies then we cannot avoid the responsibility of leadership. In these situations leadership means holding the attitude and focus—love, clarity, openness, whatever is appropriate—and, simply by example, being a beacon that guides the other people into working with and in the same energy field. Again, this is why it is useful to prepare carefully in advance. There are very few people who can

17

walk off the street and straight into leading a ceremony and hold a clear resonance; whereas careful prior meditation and contemplation, and having at least an hour (some people would suggest days) to oneself before the ceremony, greatly ease effective and graceful leadership.

Setting Up and Cleansing the Space

The space in which the ceremony takes place needs to be clear, clean and purified. This purification is both visible and invisible.

I shall describe the format for cleansing which I use and which, in one way or another, is more or less a standard operating procedure. It is very simple and involves three stages. Incidentally, this technique can, of course, be used regularly in your home or workplace, and not just for ostensibly sacred events. The three stages are: First, meditate in the place and attune to it. Second, physically clean it. Third, spiritually cleanse it.

Attunement to the Space

Before I work in a space I sit in it and become familiar with its vibrations. I attune to the place as a living being. There is life in every atom of its structure.

Before a ceremony I sit in its location, relax and bring myself to centre. I then have a real conversation with the place, saying that we are coming to celebrate there, asking permission and saying that I want to clean and to cleanse it. I sit there for a while, just waiting, my meditative mind receptive to any impressions it might catch. I then look around carefully and sum up the physical cleaning that is needed, and any changes required for the celebration. Before I leave, I thank the location and, if it is a place outdoors, I usually offer it a gift. In some traditions it is usual to give some grain or tobacco. If I have forgotten to bring a special gift, I usually give or bury some money.

Physical Cleaning of the Place

It is then necessary physically to clean the place. This has to be done with care, patience and love. Working in this way, we actually put vibrations of care and love into the atomic substance of the location.

Inner Cleansing and Purification

Having attuned to the location and physically cleaned it, we now need to make certain that its inner energy and atmosphere are as we want them. If you have a regular meditation practice, then it might be enough for you simply to go and meditate for a long period in the location; you sit in silence waiting until you feel that your meditative calm and radiance have filled the atmosphere of the place.

The Four Elements

Even though I spend much time in meditation, I also always use some simple inner technology. My first strategy for inner cleansing is to balance and align the energies using an ancient but very straightforward method. This method places an object representative of each of the four elements in each of the four corners of the space. If the space does not have four easily identifiable corners, I place the objects in the best way that I can. It is not important that the objects are placed exactly in the pattern of a square; the *intent* of going for the four corners is what matters. For each of the objects I usually use:

A bowl of salt representing *Earth*.
A bowl of water representing *Water*.
Smoking incense representing *Air*.
A lit candle representing *Fire*.

Just place the objects in each of the four corners, and then wait and sense the atmosphere settle and change. It does not matter in which order or position the elements are placed—though some people, from various traditions, do keep to a particular order. Nor is it necessary to place the elements with any ceremony. If you have a child, she may enjoy placing them. (This works perfectly to settle a room after an argument or after chaotic visitors have left. You can also do the four corners of your house.)

If you want an image that will help you appreciate the efficacy of this method, imagine in your mind's eye an ancient temple. In each of the four corners of the temple is a huge tripod, at least five feet high, holding a very large bowl. In one bowl there is Earth. In the second bowl, Water. In the third, Air. In the fourth, Fire. The four together set the tone and quality for the whole temple.

The location of these four elements in the four corners immediately sets up an archetypal resonance which settles the atmosphere. Each representative of an element attracts unto itself the energy of its archetype. As all four are working together, all four elemental archetypes are attracted in a square of equilibrium.

Blessing Incense and Candles

A burning candle possesses a natural atmosphere of sacred calm and can transform an atmosphere. To leave a candle burning for a long time in a particular place, perhaps for days or weeks or months, always helps to settle and enhance atmosphere. In a different way, incense—providing you use an appropriate fragrance—also cleanses and enhances.

It is useful in cleansing work to bless the candle and incense. When we bless an object, we deliberately radiate into its atomic structure the energy and atmosphere of love or grace or enlightenment. If a candle has been blessed, then when it burns it will continually radiate out the quality with which it was blessed. As each atom of the wax and wick transform into flame, so its blessing is released.

20

The basic technique for blessing is very straightforward. You need to be quiet, centred and aligned. Having achieved this focused calm, you then contemplate a divine being or divine quality which, for you, represents love and perfection. Think of this being or state of consciousness and sense its energy, its blessing, coming gently down through your head and into your body. The atmosphere then comes down through your hands and radiates out through your palms.

Sense the radiation from the palms of your hands and allow it to enter into the candles or incense (or anything else which you wish to bless.) If you want, you can say some words aloud that describe what you are doing and that put power into your breath. Usually the form of these words will be something like: *In the name of the Beloved, I bless this candle.* Instead of the word 'Beloved' you can, of course, substitute the name of the perfect being or consciousness with whom you have a relationship. The only advantage to using a word such as 'Beloved' is that it does not exclude or press buttons in people from other religious belief systems.

Hold your focus on the object you are blessing until you sense and intuit that you have done the job successfully. It will not normally take more than a minute and may only take a few seconds.

There is no way that you can do any harm with this kind of blessing. If you are in any way doing something wrong, then you will feel some form of tension in your body. If you feel any tension anywhere in your body as you are doing a blessing, then you can know for certain that you have lost your spiritual focus and that you are working with materialistic personality energy. The experience of blessing needs to be graceful. The blessing energy then anchors into the molecules, cells and etheric body of the object.

Having blessed incense in this way it can be a very lovely experience to walk with it burning around the location,

21

allowing its smoke and fragrance to revitalise, soothe and cleanse the atmosphere.

As you do the blessing or walk with the incense, you may instinctively feel that you want to make blessing gestures with your hand. Again, providing that you feel calm and spiritually centred, follow your instinct; but if you feel that you are being confused by an uncertain or theatrical aspect of your personality, then stay with simplicity.

Making Holy Water

Sprinkling holy water is a classical procedure for cleansing. Making holy water is a longer process than simply blessing, because its purpose is *actively* to disperse negative and inert energy. This means that holy water must possess an inherent cleansing dynamism.

Place in front of you a bowl of water and a bowl of salt. Then bring yourself to a point of calm and alignment. Think of and place yourself in resonance with what for you is a perfect being and place your right hand out to bless the water. Imagine the energy and atmosphere of this perfect being flowing down through you and through your hand. Stay calm, grounded and relaxed.

The form of wording which I use for making holy water is old fashioned, but I like it. It addresses the salt and water as if they were living creatures—as indeed, both etherically and and sub-atomically, they are. We also need to move our hands as we do the blessing.

The hand movement which I use is that of the equal-armed cross. Moving my hand, I draw the equal-armed cross with the energy that is coming out of the palm of my right hand and I project it into the water or the salt. I sense the energy radiating from my hand and then project it into the salt whilst moving my hand to make the sign of the cross—top to bottom, then left to right; back to centre and start again.

I project several crosses from the palm of my hand as I

say the words. The actual *shape* of the cross resonates in such a way as to place it vibrationally in touch with the archetypal cross and the protective energies that are associated with it. (If you resonate with a different tradition you may choose to use, for example, instead of the cross, the five pointed star/pentagram or the symbol for OM.) In my experience the cross works perfectly. As it is an equal-armed cross it belongs to many traditions and there need be no associations with crucifixion.

So, aligned and with your hand punctuating your words by drawing the sign of the cross with the energy radiating through your palm, say:

In the name of the Beloved (affirming your alignment) I exorcise thee, (+) O creature of Salt, of all influences of evil (+) and negativity (+), so that wherever you are scattered (+), all evil (+) and negativity (+) may depart.

Pause.

In the name of the Beloved (affirming your alignment) I exorcise thee, (+) O creature of Water, of all influences of evil (+) and negativity (+), so that wherever you are scattered, all evil (+) and negativity (+) may depart.

Then, using your fingers, carefully release some of the salt into the water, again drawing the sign of the cross. Do this three times.

The water is now dynamised and will hold its potency for some time. If you switch on your poetic imagination or inner sensitivity and focus on the freshly made holy water, you may perceive that every molecule is sparkling with a light-filled cross.

Usually I use the water immediately for the cleansing work and whatever is left I return to the earth. I use either my finger or a piece of wood to scatter the water. Sprinkle it everywhere. Children like scattering the water.

Loud Noise

Finally, a brief word about using loud noise. There may be occasions when you feel that an atmosphere is simply 'stuck' in a room; or there may be occasions when you have created an atmosphere which you sense is 'sticky' and you want quickly to dismiss; equally, if you are a therapist, healer or counsellor, you may want to dismiss the atmosphere of one client before a new client comes into your space. In these instances, loud noise can be used to shake up the vibrations and unlock anything static.

I always know when my partner has completed a session with a client, because I hear her clapping loudly to dismiss the atmosphere. Resonant drums or music with a deep bass have a similar effect. You can sense the vibration of the noise entering into the fabric of a location and releasing locked-in atmospheres. We can, of course, enhance the work of the noise by actively visualising or sensing new vibrations working with the sound. Some people sound out the OM to achieve this effect.

Having done all this, you can then use the four elements and holy water to complete the process.

Blessing Food

If you can bless candles, water or incense, you can bless anything. It is simply a matter of aligning and then actively allowing the graceful energy to flow down and through you. If you want, you can do this for your food, enhancing its vitality. For some reason or other—probably because I am happy to be satisfying my hungry body—I always do this blessing with great enthusiasm. I make my inner alignment and then I thank Gaia, I thank the source of the food, I thank the cosmos for the pranic vitality, I thank the cook—and I bless the food.

Or in other immortal words: Over the teeth, over the

gums, look out, stomach, here it comes!

We can turn everything into a ceremony of blessing, bringing into every aspect of our lives an awareness of its spiritual dimensions. Blessing becomes a tool, then, in aligning us to be conscious every moment

Part Two
Birth, Marriage & Death

In this section are the scripts of three ceremonies: Welcoming, Wedding and Death. The first two rituals were requested and written for specific events. I then wrote the death ceremony following my own father's death.

If you choose to work with these particular ceremonies, then feel completely free to adjust, change and rearrange the text as you see fit. Cut, edit, substitute and transpose. Use your own prayers, invocations, addresses and affirmations. Bring in your own traditions, culture and history.

For some readers, the text may simply act as a trigger for the writing of completely new ceremonies. We have perfect freedom to create.

The style of these three ceremonies attempts to be pure, rhythmic and disciplined; and as such they may seem too serious and 'spiritual' for some readers. Despite having written them myself, I am sympathetic to this reaction, because I know that ceremonies and sacred events can be ruined by pomposity and ecclesiastical conceit. There is, I believe, a real place in ceremony for a form of childlike chaos—which has a purity all of its own. I would rather have chaos than pomposity. And above all, I would have love—in whatever form it manifests.

3
Naming & Christening

The purpose of this ceremony is to welcome a soul into human incarnation. It has two parts. In the first the soul's new body is named and introduced to its parents and godparents; and in the second an energy connection is made between the infant and a pure source of unconditional love. The ceremony ends with the child being blessed and given first a flower and then a candle to hold.

During the naming a small amount of holy water is poured onto the child's forehead. This serves two purposes. It awakens the infant to the ceremony and opens the child's attention to the name which is being given to it; to be exact the child's attention is drawn to the vibrations of its name as it is spoken. In many cultures it is considered good luck if the child cries when its forehead is made wet. This is not said simply to reassure the distressed parents; it also acknowledges that the child's attention is fully present.

In the second part of the ceremony, the celebrant draws his hand down the child's energy body and asks that it be open in order to be connected to a source of pure love and protection. This part of the ceremony is the most delicate and gentle event. It needs to be done as lightly as a feather, as if two souls were embracing. Indeed, it works because the child's soul gives the celebrant's soul permission so to work.

Also, in this part of the ceremony the celebrant is not free to choose to make a connection with any being or consciousness he wants. The connection must be with the Being of absolute compassion and love, whose energy is completely protective. In the West this Being is usually called Christ, or Messiah by the Jews, or Imam Mahdi, the

Beloved, by Muslims. In the East this Being is Krishna and the Bhodisattva Buddha. This Being, of course, has other names in other cultures.

According to esoteric tradition, the Christ created a special reservoir of energy for use in intercession and ceremonies of this kind. Through the christening the infant's body is connected permanently with this reservoir regardless of the infant's future circumstances or behaviour. It is a permanent connection to grace upon which the child can draw when in need.

Preparation

First, make a safe and sacred space. You need a special candle and a special flower which the infant can hold. You also need a small bowl of water, preferably from a well or place which you hold sacred; otherwise holy water that you have made will do. It is very pleasant to have many candles available of which only some are already alight. It is particularly good if everyone present has a candle to hold.

The whole ceremony is spoken directly to the child and done very gently. If you do not feel confident that you can celebrate it gracefully, then have someone else do it for you.

The Ceremony

Let the infant be held by whomever the parents choose; it can, of course, be one of the parents.

Greeting
Dear and beautiful being, we welcome you and we honour your presence.

You have chosen to manifest in this form, in this incarnation, and we celebrate this cycle of your existence.

Light candles.
We too are Spirit in human incarnation and thus we recognise the purpose and dynamic of your life. Our work together is to bring about the perfect unfoldment of love.

But the path of incarnation is full of learning and of challenge, and traditional wisdom has given us certain fundamental blessings for greeting every new life.

The first of these is the blessing and the naming of your human form, your body, with water.

The second is the anchoring into your life of a pure ray of unconditional love, compassion and protection.

Naming
Touching the child's head with water:
With this holy water, I bless you.
With this water, you are named _____.

Parents step forward
_____ **and** _____ **are your parents and have given you your physical body. They will care for you and nurture you.**
Each parent may now say and share anything they wish.

Godparents step forward

_____ and _____ are your godparents. They are symbolic of the spiritual beings who will always care for your spiritual unfoldment.

Each godparent may now say and share anything they wish.

Christening

With infinite wisdom and compassion, it has been ordained that all children may be blessed with a ray of pure unconditional love, compassion and protection anchored into their being.

Pass right hand from etheric crown to feet of the child; the hand should be about six inches away from the body and should move with the lightness of a feather.

Be thou open.

Perfectly aligned with the Christ energies, channel unconditional love, compassion and protection. Place your hand first on the etheric head, then on the etheric heart, then on the etheric base of the spine, allowing the Christ Light gently to anchor at each point. The hand rests at each location for only a few seconds. The atmosphere is pure grace.

Then pass your hand back up from the feet to the crown of the infant.

Be thou closed.

Life Blessing

Place a flower in the infant's hand.

Hold now this flower—emblematic of the grace and beauty that will be with you always through this life.

Place a lighted candle in the infant's hand.

Hold now this candle—emblematic of the clear spiritual purpose and protection that will be with you always through your life.

_____ (name of child), we bless you and we accept the blessing of your presence.

4
Wedding

One of the features of the emerging culture is our uncertainty about relationships and the rules that govern them. There seem to be two opposing dynamics at work at the moment, both of them stemming from spiritual impulse. The first dynamic makes us look for partnerships which provide the right context for personal and spiritual growth. This is leading to a renaissance of marriage as a sacramental relationship.

The other dynamic recognises that the situations which are appropriate for spiritual growth change from time to time—and this includes marriage. When the once-appropriate relationship has fulfilled its purpose, there comes the distress, anxiety and conflict of separation.

These two dynamics create a difficult point of tension. At one end of the spectrum we may cling on to relationships, not recognising the end of mutual growth. At the other end, we may jump out of relationships the moment that they become too challenging—no matter in what shape that challenge arises. For many people there is also the very poignant reality of children and the necessity to respect their needs and rights; there is also, to my mind, the need to avoid the social, material and emotional injustice of single parenthood.

To balance the freedom to pursue one's spiritual growth with the responsibility of an adult relationship is difficult. In my own life I have behaved in ways that I regret.

It was, therefore, with an awareness of these paradoxes and problems that I originally sat down to help create the following wedding ceremony. I wondered if my awareness of all the shadow aspects would trigger an uncreative cynicism. In the event, as I sat down to write, I was helped both by the characters of the two people for whom I was writing the ceremony and also by my own deep belief in the reality of nurturing relationships that honour sacred realities. The couple for whom I wrote the ceremony, Roger Buck and Manuela Andolina, are two very beautiful people who, to their surprise, found themselves in a relationship that worked. They are both deep meditators and totally committed to the path of spiritual unfoldment. The beginnings of their relationship were in meditation and in spiritual discussion around the book *A Course in Miracles*.

And so it was that, even with a full awareness of the shadow aspects and very real problems, the ceremony was written. It attempts to address both the physical and the spiritual aspects of marriage.

There are three points in the ceremony when the couple give each other gifts—a flower, a kiss and a lighted candle—and at these points make special pledges to each other. There is also a form of communion at the end which the couple shares with everyone present. These features allow the couple great creativity of expression through the ritual.

In many ways, it is a 'high' ceremony and needs to be done carefully and with a real sacred focus. It may be too 'high' for some people, but we felt a real need, given the problems of relationship, to make a powerful and serious spiritual statement about marriage.

The Ceremony

For the ceremony you need: a small tray with broken bread; a small salt container; a chalice; a small water jug and a small wine jug; two flowers; two candles in holders.

The sanctuary or sacred space should be arranged as the couple want. It works well if all the guests are in a circle with the couple in the centre, kneeling or sitting cross-legged and facing each other. The celebrant then sits at right angles to them, facing their profiles.

When everyone else is already present, the couple come in and sit apart.

(1) Attunement
Celebrant: **Let us take five minutes' silence and each of us in our own private way bring ourselves with loving awareness fully here.**

Five minutes' silence.

(2) Prayer
The people say a prayer together that the couple have chosen. It is perhaps best to use a general invocation or blessing. Make certain that if people do not know the prayer, you have it copied and circulated.

The couple now come and kneel or sit facing each other.

(3) Preamble
Celebrant: **We are here today to bear witness to, to bless and to receive the blessing of _____ 's and _____ 's marriage.**

Marriage is when two people, responding to the most profound human instinct for companionship and intimacy, commit themselves to a unique and intimate partnership in life.

This commitment is woven together with trust, with

support and with fidelity.

It is based in love, in affection and in an instinctive bonding between two people.

This bonding is of the physical body, is of the human personality and is of the inner spiritual being.

Pause

But let us be self-aware of the challenges.

Marriage is the most intense of human relationships. This intensity derives from all the dynamic qualities of human incarnation, of human karma and of human unfoldment into perfect love.

In the closeness and intimacy of your relationship, your partner symbolises for you the relationship between yourself and the whole of humanity. Your partner represents, both in reality and in projection, all the facets of your potential for relationship.

Where you sow or expect hurt, misunderstanding, rejection or isolation, so you will find it in each other. But where you sow or expect love, trust, generosity, support and affection, so you will find love, trust, generosity, support and affection in each other.

You need to be serious about the work that marriage entails. Be aware that in marriage—of all the relationships you may have—there is the need for strength, generosity and love as you prove yourselves part of a cosmos unfolding to perfect love.

Know that when you love each other perfectly, you will have grown to loving all life perfectly.

(4) Alignment with the Highest
Celebrant: Let us now lift up our hearts and our consciousness. Let us bring into our awareness the highest ideals of love and of marriage—and let these ideals incarnate now in this time and place.

Dear and Overlighting Spirit, Beloved of All Life, Heart

of Compassion, open our lives and our understanding to the full potential of marriage—of human trust, support and fidelity. In this most fundamental of human relationships, allow us to see and to experience the inner spiritual dynamic which guides all life to the unfoldment of perfect love.

(5) The couple choose a piece of music to be played here.

(6) Gaia Blessing
Celebrant: Let us now invoke the blessing of Gaia.
Let us be aware of our Mother the Earth—of her care, of her embrace, of her nurture.
Mother of all life,
Ocean of creation,
Draw us deep into the waves of your embrace.
Bless this couple with health, with strength and with the nurturing warmth of true growth.
_____, _____—Open your lives to each other.

(7) Gift of a Flower and First Pledge
Wife gives husband a flower.
Wife: **With this flower, I . . .** (She makes a pledge/promise to her husband.)
Husband gives wife a flower.
Husband: **With this flower, I . . .** (He makes a pledge/ promise to his wife.)

(8) Cupid's Blessing
Celebrant: Let us now invoke the blessing of the Angel of Lovers.
Cupid/Eros—we ask for and acknowledge your presence here.
Weaver of hearts.
Alchemist of romance.

Tender kiss of all life.
Bless this marriage with your spiritual grace.
Let the healing of sacred romance ever bless this marriage.

_____ , _____ —Open your hearts to each other.

(9) Gift of a Kiss and Second Pledge

Wife gives husband a kiss.

Wife: **With this kiss, I . . . .** (Wife makes a pledge to her husband.)

Husband gives wife a kiss.

Husband: **With this kiss, I . . . .** (Husband makes a pledge to his wife.)

(10) Angel of the Home's Blessing

Celebrant: **Let us now invoke the blessing of the Angel of the Home.**

We invoke and we acknowledge the presence of the overlighting Angel of the Home.

Blessed Angel of the Home who loves and understands all the complex dynamics of human relationship—bless this marriage with your presence, forever drawing their love and their actions into their perfect potential.

Bless their home so that they always reside in a sanctuary of perfectly unfolding love.

_____ , _____ —Open your lives' purpose to each other.

(11) Gift of a Candle and Third Pledge

Wife lights her candle and gives it to husband.

Wife: **With this candle, I . . . .** (Wife makes a pledge to her husband.)

Husband lights his candle and gives it to wife.

Husband: **With this candle, I . . . .** (Husband makes a pledge to his wife.)

(12) Prayer and affirmation
The couple now say a prayer together.
Wife: **I offer myself as your wife.**
Husband: **I offer myself as your husband.**

(13) Silence. Or the couple may choose another piece of music or a poem, prayer or piece of prose.

(14) Love Feast and Couple's Blessing
Husband and wife: **In recognition of our physical union, we scatter salt upon this bread.**

There is a small tray with broken bread upon it on to which the couple scatter a small amount of salt. They then bless it with their hands.

There is one chalice into which the couple simultaneously pour water and wine from separate containers.

Husband and wife: **In recognition of our spiritual union, we mix water with this wine.**

They then bless the water/wine.
The couple taste the bread and wine. They then share the feast with everyone present. The couple walk around the sacred space, one with the bread, the other with the wine/water. This is also an opportunity to receive and to give individual blessings and wishes. Having completed the sharing, the couple come back to their original places.

(15) Recognition and Final Blessing
Celebrant: **On behalf of everyone and every being here present, I say that we recognise you, _____ and_____ , as wife and husband.**

May the Beloved in all loving kindness bless you and be with you in your marriage.

May strength and purposefulness sustain you and bring you great spiritual growth together.

May wisdom bring you enlightenment and patient clarity.

And may perfect love shine ever through your lives.

(16) Music or silence and then exit.

A Note on Divorce

It would be naive and unrealistic to ignore the reality that couples divorce. A time may come when the rhythm of creative partnership and mutual growth ends, and it may then be appropriate for the couple to separate. This has been the experience for many of us. It does not invalidate the beauty and the commitments of the wedding ceremony. No commitment, no wedding, should be a prison.

The problem, of course, is in knowing whether it truly is right to separate and that we are not avoiding a lesson by running away from the relationship. Equally, the problem is to separate with grace. I have remorse as I contemplate the manner of the ending of two of my own relationships, but out of my regret and my attempts to learn the lessons of the process, I think a certain clarity is possible about the conduct of separation.

The answer is simple. In our marriages we need to communicate truthfully with each other about everything. We need to be able to speak honestly and we need to be able to listen and hear clearly and realistically. Too often we are afraid to talk candidly with our partner, unable to express honesty and fearing rejection. In the same way, we are unable to hear what our partner says to us—or we hear it and, in doing so, we react so fast and so emotionally that we never truly understand and respond to the message.

No relationship is perfect and in all relationships there are times when one or both partners are alienated, unhappy and thinking about flight. We need to talk about it all as we feel it. We need to make it safe to talk honestly. If alienation and the possibility of separation are not forbidden areas of communication, then many problems will melt. If there is ongoing regular and honest communication, then a potential separation will be spotted many months, perhaps years, in advance. It can be talked over and examined as between two friends, and the emotional dynamics defused and melted into trust. This form of open dialogue can also be deeply helped if the couple regularly meditate together and allow an open heart resonance of love to pass between them.

In separation there is no way of avoiding pain. For two close friends, creatures who have slept together and warmed each other, to separate will hurt. But if there is calm, grounded communication it can happen without the chaos, anger and self-pity of so many divorces.

There is also the practical and occult problem that the couple will still be linked by threads of energy and these need to be cut. I recommend Phyllis Krystal's book *Cutting the Ties that Bind,* which provides exercises for this kind of separation.

In public, the partners may wish to acknowledge their gratitude to each other and to honour the growth and gifts of their time together. The clean and happy end of a marriage may, in fact, be a liberating release signalling a celebration and party.

If children are involved, then at least this form of separation means that the parents can be creatively cooperative. And, indeed, after a separation conducted in this manner, couples may choose to stay together, sacrificing their individual freedom to honour their responsibility to their children. What is wisdom, however, rests in the dynamic of each individual situation.

5
Death

There are obviously certain challenges in writing a ritual for death. Unlike birth and marriage, death is not associated with celebration in our culture. Death is a mystery for most people—and mystery evokes anxiety, superstition and caution. Equally, death is associated with pain, sadness, disaster and loss.

Any ceremonial approach to death, therefore, requires care and sensitivity. It needs to be based both in detachment and in a completely accepting love.

Because of the sensitivity of the subject, before leading rituals around death we need to be certain that our attitude is balanced and fully aware of the inner realities. If, for example, we do not fully accept that death is just the doorway to another reality, as consciousness is released from physical life, then we should leave rituals of death alone and find a friend or colleague to lead them.

At birth, we recognised the coming into incarnation of a soul, the manifestation of a higher or inner self. We greeted this arrival and we blessed the new body of the incarnating consciousness. At marriage, we recognised that the wedding was not simply a three-dimensional event between two personalities, but a multi-dimensional commitment between two inner consciousnesses seeking to grow and to travel the spiritual path together.

At death, we become aware of the rhythm that draws souls in and out of incarnation. The learning processes of a lifetime have reached completion and the inner self has chosen to be attracted back to an existence within the greater soul of all life. This one cycle of learning, this one lifetime, is now complete and the soul withdraws. In a much smaller daily rhythm, we all leave our physical bodies at night and exist in the multi-dimensional world of the inner planes—and then return to this reality. At death, we leave our temporary bodies to enter the inner planes for a longer period. This is the greater rhythm of incarnation and it holds no fear for us; it holds only the process of our spiritual unfoldment. We incarnate and, within the constraints of physical existence, learn the lessons of love and wisdom. And then we remove ourselves from incarnation.

Death is a release into the clarity of pure contemplation. There is no longer the confusion of incarnate human existence. Now we can truly see and it is no longer through a veil.

The complete human personality exists as consciousness after death. It has lost only its dense physical form. After a long period of time, the emotional and mental aspects of the personality are withdrawn into the memory of the soul—and the soul remembers its previous incarnation as if it were the chords and descants of music that has been played. The soul now reflects on that music and contemplates a new music for a new lifetime.

Some deaths, however, occur violently: in accidents and in war, in murder and suicide. We cannot ignore the tragedy of these fatalities or be insensitive to the shocked feelings of the bereaved. But we need to remember that the essence of the process of death and rebirth remains the same. It is still a multi-dimensional and spiritual process. If we are close to a violent death, then we need to take on an attitude that is self-disciplined and philosophical. This is not to say that we do not acknowledge, express and heal our grief. But if we are to act as our own celebrants and as our own priests, then we have no choice but to hold a self-discipline based in courage, love and compassion.

Acknowledging the true inner realities can in itself bring us comfort.

In dealing with other people, however, who are suffering a violent bereavement, my advice is never to counsel them with multi-dimensional common sense. Do not comfort with words that spin from an active mind aware of 'spiritual' truths. Focus in the heart. Be love and compassion.

In working with death we need to be aware that we are working with three distinct situations:

a) The departure of a personality and soul.
b) The elimination of the dead physical body.
c) The disorientation, loss and grief of the departed's family, friends and colleagues.

It is beyond the remit of this book to counsel and to give advice on bereavement. I suggest, though, that people who are drawn to lead these ceremonies take their pastoral role seriously and read books on death and bereavement such as those by Elisabeth Kübler-Ross.

Before discussing and describing an appropriate ceremony for death, it is necessary first of all to look at the state and consciousness of the dying individual. Again, this book is not the place for a full and adequate discussion concerning the process of dying—I would recommend as essential reading Chapters Five, Six and Seven of Alice Bailey's *Esoteric Healing*, which deal specifically with dying and death. It is, however, possible to make a few comments which may help.

Unless the dying individual is a committed knower of spiritual realities, then death is a great and bewildering mystery. Furthermore, there may be conflict between an elemental will-to-survive in the physical body and the soul's choice to disincarnate. The individual may, therefore, be confused and truculent. Whilst engaged in this process of surrendering to death, the dying person may be difficult to help. All we can do is to listen, to comfort and to love. In nearly all cases, however, there comes a time at the very end—perhaps hours or perhaps days or even months before transition—when the individual begins to experience a calm surrender to the situation. At this point, it may well be appropriate for the individual to receive a final blessing—*but in a form that she can accept.* Let her choose, if she wishes, to receive a priest or minister from a religion with which she feels associated. I am worried that over-enthusiastic members of the new age culture may attempt, blatantly or subtly, to impose ideas or ceremonies which are alien to the dying person. All that matters during the time of dying is an actively expressed love from the heart —not words.

If the dying individual trusts you and shares your belief system, then there are certain things that can be done to facilitate the process. Have at least one candle always alight and do what is right to achieve a sacred space around the person. It is taught in esoteric Buddhism—which contains a sophisticated science of helping the dying—that the colour orange facilitates the disengagement of the consciousness from the physical body. It also teaches that of all the scents, sandalwood is the most suitable because its inherent vibration is dynamic and facilitates separation. Beware of scents, sounds and colours—as well as emotions and thoughts—which tend to bind the consciousness or hold back its release. In death we are cutting the greatest tie that binds. Read to your friend transcendental passages with which you know she is in tune. Play the music she loves. Hold an attitude of joyful release.

After the actual death, be aware that the personality and consciousness of the deceased are still fully in existence and often still close to the physical body. Person by person, the appropriate atmosphere will vary, but in the vast majority of cases this final breaking of the tie with the physical body is indeed a blessed and joyful release. It is a perfect opportunity to meditate upon the inner reality of existence.

Immediately following the death, the most important

thing is that we hold an attitude of loving detachment and that we do not radiate any emotional or thought currents which might hold back the newly released consciousness.

It is important now also to be practical and to realise that, whilst the consciousness of the discarnate soul continues, we also have a dead body on our hands. It is strongly advised that arrangements are made in advance for cremation and not burial. Cremation is a fast and fiery way to facilitate the cutting of any ties or magnetic attractions that may hold back the discarnate consciousness. Also a dead body decays in a way that is neither attractive nor ecologically useful; if possible, therefore, avoid burials which pollute the earth or long delays in disposing of the body.

Because the physical body begins to decay very fast, it is important to sprinkle it with holy water and also to bless it with incense. This will help to hold the atmosphere around it clean and sacred. Leave a candle or candles alight near the body and place appropriate religious symbols around it. Release the body to the undertakers. Until new age funeral services begin to appear, we have no choice but to trust the current funeral companies. Most of them perform a quick, efficient and dignified service.

Again, it is worth reminding ourselves that we can use death as an inspiration for contemplation and deep insight. When death is close to us we are in a situation where the veil between the two worlds is very thin. The dying individual moves directly between the two worlds and as our thoughts follow the released consciousness so we ourselves become seers. Many people experience new dimensions of sensitivity, telepathy and intuition when they are close to a friend's death. Unreality gives way to reality as we perceive the mysterious continuum of all existence.

There are two images which may help us adopt the right attitude.

The first image is that of the philosopher with a human skull upon his desk. This is not a macabre image, but one of a mystic acknowledging reality. All things must pass.

The second image is that of Buddhist contemplatives meditating in graveyards and near funeral pyres. Again, this is no sinister exercise but the flowering recognition of the natural transience of all life.

The Ceremony

This ritual is written to take place in the chapel alongside a crematorium.

Make certain that there are candles and some sandalwood incense burning. If you can arrange it, place three major candles in a triangle around the coffin. Arrange matters with the chapel so that there is no sense of urgency about the proceedings and you are not rushed. It may in certain circumstances, therefore, be better to do this full ceremony before going to the crematorium.

Have everyone present make a circle around the coffin.

Let us take five minutes' silence and each of us, in our own way, come to centre and to attunement.

I suggest you now read a statement which makes clear the realities of death. Immediately below are two examples: the first from my own introduction to this section; the second from the Tibetan teacher Djwahl Khul.

'At death, we become aware of the rhythm that draws souls in and out of incarnation. The learning processes of a lifetime have reached completion and the soul has chosen to be attracted back to an existence within the Greater Soul of All Life. This one small cycle of learning is now complete and it withdraws. At night, we all leave our bodies and exist in the world of the inner planes —and then return to this reality. At death, we leave our temporary bodies to enter the inner planes for a longer period. This is the greater rhythm of incarnation and it holds no fear for us; it holds only the process of our spiritual unfoldment.

51

Death is a release into the clarity of pure contemplation. There is no longer the confusion of incarnate human existence. Now we can truly see and it is no longer through a veil.

The complete human personality exists as consciousness after death. It has lost only its dense physical form, the elements of which are returned to its parent, Gaia. After a long period of time, the emotional and mental aspects of the personality are withdrawn into the memory of the soul—and the soul remembers its previous incarnation as if it were the chords and descants of music that has been played. The soul now reflects on that music and contemplates a new music for a new lifetime.'

'Death, if we could but realise it, is one of our most practised activities. We have died many times and shall die again and again. Death is essentially a matter of consciousness. We are conscious one moment on the physical plane, and a moment later we have withdrawn onto another plane and are actively conscious there. Just as long as our consciousness is identified with the form aspect, death will hold for us its ancient terror. Just as soon as we know ourselves to be souls, and find that we are capable of focusing our consciousness or sense of awareness in any form or on any plane at will, or in any direction within the form of God, we shall no longer know death.' (From: Alice Bailey, *A Treatise on White Magic*, Lucis Press, p.494)

Dear friends, sisters, brothers, we are here today to honour and to celebrate the passing over from this reality of our dear friend and sister _____.

This is a time of mystery—and a time of sadness and of joy.

The mystery derives from the thinning of the veils between our world and the inner world of spirit—from a clear sense that, although we cannot see it, there is a complete continuation of life.

Our sadness comes from the loss of a personality whom we shall never see again in physical form.

Our joy comes from the knowledge of her release from physical incarnation into the world of inner contemplation and of spirit.

Let us honour and be aware of all these profound elements in this moment: the mystery, the sadness and the celebration.

Pause

'Behold, I show you a mystery: there is a natural body and there is a spiritual body; for this corruptible must put on incorruption and this mortal must put on immortality. So when this corruptible shall have put on incorruption and this mortal shall have put on immortality, then shall be brought to pass the saying that is written: Death is swallowed up in victory. O death, where is thy sting? O grave, where is thy victory?' (From: *The Bible*, First Epistle of St Paul the Apostle to the Corinthians, Verse 51)

Dear and departed friend, we thank you for bringing us together. Here in the presence of your discarded earthly veil—yet still aware of your full presence in consciousness—we cannot believe only in the illusion of material existence.

Your death leads us from illusion to reality.
Your death leads us from darkness to light.
Your death leads us from untruth to truth.
Pause.

The purpose of all incarnation is to bring spirit and love more fully into existence.

Spirit organises and brings all matter into life. It has its tides and rhythms—some short and simple, some long and complex.

53

Here, in your life, dear _____, we have experienced spirit at work and in its full* rhythm you have chosen now to withdraw. You leave behind your earthly veil, inert, devoid of life—and you draw our attention to the inner realities. (*Delete full if the circumstances are inappropriate).

'If you would indeed behold the spirit of death, open your heart wide unto the body of life.

For life and death are one, even as the river and sea are one.' (Kahlil Gibran, *The Prophet*.)

At this point an appropriate prayer or mantram or poem is said by everyone together.

After the prayer, again silence.

Let us honour now our sadness and grief at your departure. Shortly we shall return the remains of your physical body to Gaia and it is right that we now acknowledge the depth of our feelings about you and that nothing is hidden.

We seek in no way to hold you back from the path that is now before you and we wish you only well and love.

Group Sharing

At this stage, people present in the circle may share what they feel to be appropriate. It may be poetry, prose or music. It may be an anecdote. The atmosphere should be such that people speak genuinely, simply and from the heart—and do not burble from the head. Authenticity is to be encouraged.

It may be that this part of the ceremony includes impromptu dance or singing. On the other hand, it may be quiet and sombre. Let whatever wants to happen, happen.

This part of the ceremony will come to its own natural ending.

Let the atmosphere settle.

Once it is settled, this is now the time when people can, if they wish, actually verbalise their farewells.

Again, pause for silence.

You may choose then to play a piece of music.

In life, death appears the greatest of mysteries—but death is simply life in another form.

There is no break in the great flow of existence. There is no life that is made into nothing.

Everything—from particle to cosmos—is caught in the great breath of existence, moving in experience from love to greater love, from unknowing to greater knowing. No life is outside of this cosmic flow.

If we had but the eyes to see, we would see now in these moments the movement of our departed brother/sister further into the great unfoldment.

Dear and beloved friend, you begin now a further glorious part of your great journey. We rejoice and we celebrate your departing.

The Soul's Call
'The word goes forth from soul to form:
Behind that form, I am.
Know Me.

Cherish and know and understand
The nature of the veils of life,
But know as well the One Who lives.
Know Me.

Let not the forms of nature,
Their processes and powers prevent
Thy searchings for the mystery
Which brought the mysteries to thee.

Know well the form,
But leave it joyously and search for Me.'

(From Alice Bailey, *Esoteric Psychology*, Vol. II)

Each one of us will one day follow you. The door through which you have passed, the path which now lies before you—this is our future too.

You enter now a world of contemplative spirit free from the limitations of this earthly form and human action.

The Source of All Life draws you ever towards greater love.

Love be with you.

Music

Now let the coffin be taken into the furnace; or if this is a burial, hold silence until the coffin is in the grave. You may wish to be aware of the elements that made up the body being returned to Gaia.

Let the closest relatives and friends choose how they now want to leave the chapel. There should be time and space at this point for sharing and comfort.

The next few days can be taken as a period of sustained contemplation on the mysteries and joys of existence. In the Jewish tradition, for example, this is a time of sitting quietly and humbly and speaking only from the heart. In other traditions, for example the Celtic, there is a custom of party-giving and celebration. As always, we need to follow—in perfect freedom and love—our own path.

Dissolver of Sugar

Dissolver of sugar, dissolve me,
if this is the time.
Do it gently with a touch of hand, or a look.
Every morning I wait at dawn. That's when it's happened
before.
Or do it suddenly like an execution. How else
can I get ready for death?

You breathe without a body like a spark.
You grieve, and I begin to feel lighter.
You keep me away with your arm,
but the keeping away is pulling me in.

(From Rumi,*Open Secret*, translated by John Moyne
and Coleman Barks. Threshold Books, 1984)

57

Part Three
The Lunar Cycle, Solstices, Equinoxes & Fire Festivals

6
The Lunar Cycle

Introduction

As a child, lying in the back seat of my family's car as we drove by night, I would watch the illusion of the Moon flying along behind the telegraph poles, the wires and the trees. Because of my perspective it seemed as if the Moon was the fastest flying object that I had ever seen in my life. The image was so powerful, and I had spent so long looking at it from inside the car, that lying in bed, my eyes closed, I could still see it speeding across the sky. Even now, decades later, I am surprised as I look at the night sky that the Moon is so still.

Yet she is still and her stillness is strangely haunting. Here in the black sky is this strange creature, sometimes invisible, then coyly revealing herself, a sliver of silver light growing to become a full translucent orb. And then she retreats again, withdrawing her gentle revelation.

The Moon evokes poetry and my attempt above at a few lines of poetic prose demonstrates that I too am seduced by its mystery. But it is not romantic to talk of the Moon's mystery. The light which the Moon shines, reflecting the Sun, has a strange silver quality that clothes any object on which it falls with an unusual and suggestive silver-grey veil.

The night is black without the light of the Moon—but even with that light, there are silence, shadows and a silver translucence. It is no wonder that mythology veils the Moon in female shrouds. This shimmering, watery appearance hints at other influences. And these influences are very real.

Increased Sensitivity

The magnetism of the Moon draws and controls the tides of the Earth's oceans. This magnetism, in fact, has an effect on all water wherever it is found. The magnetic pull can be felt by all living beings because their bodies all contain water. Whether the pulling sensation is recognised or not depends upon the species. Certainly there are many animals and small creatures who time their growth and migrations according to the lunar influence. This influence is also substantial upon the plant world. Gardeners through the ages have realised that planting, pruning and cultivating can be enhanced by recognising the effect of the lunar rhythm.

There is also the definite influence which the lunar cycle has upon the human psyche. Scientific psychological studies have demonstrated the powerful effect of this cycle upon human behaviour, the full Moon coinciding with more extreme anxiety, tension, sensitivity and other pathological conditions. Stories of werewolves are symbolic of the fact that at the time of the full Moon it is more difficult for people to keep their shadow aspects disciplined, repressed or sublimated.

The hidden reason for this heightened psychic activity has always been known to students of esoteric philosophy. In the same way that the Moon magnetically influences water, so it also affects the more subtle—or 'etheric'—body of the human being. The full Moon increases the vibratory rate of the etheric body. This is experienced by many people as a direct physical sensation that makes them, on the positive side, more physically speedy and energised, and on the negative side, more anxious and nervy.

This increase in the vibratory rate of the etheric body is extremely important. It is important because the etheric body connects the dense physical body with all the more subtle planes of existence. And it not only connects the physical body with the inner planes, it also acts as a protector and filter. This is especially important in relation to the human brain and nervous and glandular systems.

The human brain, the nervous system and the glands which feed the endocrine system are all interwoven and protected by etheric webs. These webs, which are similar to spiders' webs, act as protective filters, blocking or toning down energy from the more subtle, higher-vibrational inner planes. This means that no inner-plane energy or information can anchor down into the human body, particularly into the brain, nervous and glandular systems, without passing through the etheric webs. More than that, the different regions of the physical brain itself, each with its own specific function, are divided from each other by etheric webs. These internal webs prevent information from spilling over from one region of the brain into another. This is vital to mental health, particularly in the areas of the brain which are concerned with unconscious and subconscious dynamics; to maintain psychological stability it is crucial that the different types of information in the various regions of the brain do not bleed into one another. Then the whole brain itself is protected by an etheric web.

When the etheric webs of the brain vibrate faster, they become more elastic and they allow more information to pass through them. This is precisely what happens at the time of the full Moon: the etheric webs are influenced by the Moon, vibrate faster, become more elastic and allow more inner energy and information to flow through into the human brain and nervous system.

Thus, at the full Moon, an individual may find himself prey to a flow of subconscious thoughts and information that may be quite overwhelming. Equally the individual also finds it easier to anchor down, in full self-consciousness, more information and impulses than usual from the inner spiritual world. All this means that the full Moon is a time of increased sensitivity and psychic activity. At the time of the full Moon, the veil between the two worlds thins

63

and opens.

For the unstable personality, this time creates certain difficulties. For the stable personality, however, the full Moon offers a period for more intense spiritual activity, for more profound and dynamic inner work. In fact, if you are sensitive or moving along the spiritual path, you have little choice about the increased inner activity. The big question, then, is whether to cooperate with it or not, whether to take advantage of it or ignore it.

One can see from all this how the effect of the lunar rhythm is essentially inner and subjective. There is a natural inner cycle of reflective or passive contemplation when the Moon is dark, leading up to a peak of active inner and meditative work when the Moon is full.

The Archetypal Rhythm and Global Signal

For many thousands of years mystic workers have intensified their spiritual work at the time of the full Moon. This ongoing work over such a long period means that a rhythm and pattern have been created in the inner planes, so that when we choose to work at these times we slip into their pattern. Slipping into their pattern, our work is made much easier. Like geese flying in the slip-stream of the V-shaped flock, we find that our path is made smoother, and in this case deeper, by those who have gone before us.

Moreover the full Moon is a global signal which can be seen no matter where we are upon the planet. In a society without clocks or calendars, the waxing and waning of the moon is the easiest way of marking time and in many cultures the lunar cycle has been used, like the Equinoxes and Solstices, as a widespread call for spiritual attention. In many of today's world religions, the full Moon is still used as a signal for religious festival. The Christian Easter is dated by the weekend after the first full Moon after the Spring Equinox. The Haj and Ramadan of Islam are signalled by the Moon, as is the Passover in Judaism or the

Buddha's birthday.

In a conversation I took part in a while ago it was agreed that we would really recognise that the new planetary culture had arrived when the whole planet paused—shops, schools, offices and all institutions closed—for a few days around the time of the full Moon. The full Moon would be an accepted monthly pause, as normal as the weekend or the summer vacation are now. It was even suggested that women's rhythms might attune to the Moon so that this monthly pause would allow women to withdraw from materialistic activity if they wished.

A Clear Flow of Solar Energy

A further reason that is put forward for the intensity of the full Moon concerns the Sun. When the Moon is full, it is fully reflecting the light of the Sun. This happens because the Moon is, in relation to the Earth, directly opposite the Sun. In this position, the Moon is located so as not to obscure any of the Sun's energy coming into Earth. This energy from the Sun is both physical and spiritual.

What is interesting about this particular idea is that it implies that there is a surge in energy at the time of the full Moon, but that this energy comes not from the Moon, but from the Sun.

Summary of Influences

It may be helpful to summarise the reasons why we take notice of the lunar cycle and the full Moon in particular:

* The Moon's magnetic influence, working on the etheric body, makes us much more sensitive to inner realities.
* Historically, the full Moon has been used for focused inner work; therefore, we follow in and are helped by an archetypal pattern.
* As the Moon can be seen everywhere upon the globe, it acts as a signal for the widest possible group work.

65

* Located on the opposite side of the Earth from the Sun, the full Moon allows a completely clear channel for solar energy.

Working with the Lunar Rhythm

There is such a poetic and evocative element to the cycles of the Moon, that, as I write, I find myself reluctant to lay down structures and strategies on how to work with it. There is an imaginative and creative element in all of us, and I fear that, in suggesting certain formal approaches to practical inner work and personal transformation, I might stunt, censor or disempower individual creative initiatives.

In suggesting certain clear procedures and awarenesses, I do not want to take energy away from anyone who wishes to dance with the Moon, or howl, or experiment with new ceremonies and festivities with a group. Women in particular, both historically and today, have ways of expressing themselves in relation to the Moon which are directly related to Goddess religions and the contemporary resurrection of the Female element in our society. Let every individual and group find their own way of working within our sacred environment.

If what I suggest in this book does not fit well with you, then a mixture of study, contemplation, instinct, intuition and imagination will surely take you in the appropriate direction. I am careful in suggesting a balance of study and imagination, for one without the other leads either to over-seriousness or to flightiness.

In my experience there are two kinds of work that are done with the lunar cycle. There is the work of *spiritual service* and there is the work of *personal transformation*. For both of them, the full Moon is the time for intense activity and the dark Moon is the time for contemplation and planning. Both modes of work are almost purely concerned with inner dimensions, unlike the Solar and Fire festivals which are more social and extrovert. We shall focus first on the work of spiritual service and the full Moons and then look at how the lunar rhythm can help the process of personal transformation.

Spiritual Service and the Full Moon

Like most of us I was a sensitive and imaginative child, and lived naturally in a multi-dimensional world. This world was filled with other beings and consciousnesses, and I was aware that different levels of being existed simultaneously with the one that I could see with my eyes and touch with my hands.

As I grew older I gained an increasing concern for social and natural justice and I became a political animal looking for action to redress the injustices and ills of the planet; and for a while I forgot about the inner world I had known as a child. Then, in my mid-twenties, that other world began to re-surface in my consciousness and in order to explore it fully I began to turn within. It was a natural instinct that led me into meditative silence and into contemplation of the invisible cosmos.

The political activist became a mystic. Yet I retained my sensitivity to the problems of the real world. Retaining this political awareness I was acutely conscious of accusations that I was self-obsessed, studying my navel and of no use to man or beast. This has always been the accusation of the worldly activist against the mystic: *You do nothing!*

In my experience of contemplative silence, however, I knew that the accusation was unfounded. Here in the invisible silence was the true world of causes. My dawning understanding of this reality was empowered by my reading of esoteric and spiritual philosophy where it is taught that it is the inner, invisible, multi-dimensional world which is the *real* 'real' world. What we see and touch and hear and smell and taste—this three-dimensional world—is but the appearance of the inner dynamic realities.

This inner world is one of energy that anchors down into

the form and actions which we see around us. What students of esoteric philosophy have always known is that, through inner work, it is possible to influence the outer visible world. An individual's feelings, attitudes, thoughts and inspirations affect the world just as much as her physical actions. All matter is electromagnetic energy and it can be directly influenced by what we feel or think: the energy of our feeling or thought continues; it does not simply evaporate. Furthermore, using our active imagination and concentration, we can direct feelings and thoughts. In the words of the famous adage: *Energy follows thought.*

All of this is crucial for the mystic or inner worker who is concerned with the world around him, for it means that he can work, in silence, to affect that world. Sitting quietly, good energy, 'good vibrations', can be radiated and directed to situations that require it. Even more effectively, the inner worker can attune to sources of pure healing and love, and then *invoke* love and healing to channel and radiate it.

Many people with a regular meditation practice include, as a matter of course, in their meditation a period which is devoted to radiating a healing and blessing. Of course, in many ways meditating itself is a blessing for it imparts a vibration of calmness and peace into the surrounding environment.

At the full Moon inner and meditative work is much easier for us. It is, therefore, the perfect time for an increased focus on spiritual service—the service of working with pure sources of energy to heal and facilitate the growth of all life on Earth.

The dark Moon, on the other hand, is a time for deep meditative study and contemplation. It is a time for musing and for careful introspection. It is a time of investigation and reflection. The sight or sense of the first thin crescent of the new Moon then triggers us into gear for a more active phase. Our focus becomes more outgoing and expansive. Then, as the full Moon approaches and our sensitivity begins to increase its vibration, we are called fully to the work of dynamic service.

Full Moon Meditation

There is a special form of meditation, for both individuals and groups, which has been well tried and tested by many groups and is particularly appropriate for the full Moon. This type of meditation is called *invocative meditation*. Essentially it is very simple: We tune in to what needs help. We tune in to pure sources of love and healing. We then invoke and radiate that love and healing.

So the basic meditation structure is:

1) Sit, become centred and aligned.
2) Earth and anchor.
3) Become aware of those areas and situations on the planet which are in need of help. Focus on those situations with compassion.
4) Bring your awareness back to centre and alignment.
5) Reach up in your consciousness to a pure source of love, light and healing.
6) Invoke love, light and healing to flow down from this source.
7) Radiate these energies to where they are needed.

I will now go through these stages in greater detail. If you do not meditate regularly, don't worry. This particular form of meditation has such a deliberate flow and intention to it that you will be able to do it anyway. You may have a bit of trouble with self-discipline if you are on your own, in which case you might want to find a meditation group with which to work. This form of invocative meditation might also be just the kind of practical inner service which will motivate you into a regular meditative practice.

This practice takes between ten and thirty minutes, and its format is precisely the same for groups as it is for individuals. The only addition for groups is that the people in the group need first to link with each other in an attitude of love and enlightenment.

After fully describing its structure, I will give the words that can be used to lead a group full Moon meditation.

1—Relaxed, centred and aligned

As with all meditation, we need to be completely relaxed, yet also completely awake and aware. The body, emotions and thoughts are quiet—but in the centre we are there, watching and conscious. We need to give ourselves enough time to come to a state of quiet. It is helpful to make certain that the face and stomach muscles are relaxed, and that breathing is regular and calm. It may help to exhale as far as you can, emptying the lungs even to a point of discomfort; then let the in-breath bring air deep into your lungs, relaxing the diaphragm, releasing tension and facilitating a gentle, unnoticed breathing.

In the midst of this calm personality, sitting like the Mona Lisa or a happy Buddha, is our consciousness. In most meditation the problem now is to retain a clear consciousness, focused behind the eyes and in the head. Distracting thoughts, feelings and impressions tempt one's consciousness away from being quiet and focused. In invocative meditation, however, there is work to be done and we can simply get on with it. Doing things—doing active inner work in meditation—is often the solution to the problem of a lack of concentration and a wandering mind.

Calmed and centred, we spend a while becoming aware of the quality of our inner or higher self. Most people find it easiest to do this by carefully focusing on and contemplating the area a few inches above the head (crown chakra). Just gently lift your consciousness and become aware of the region directly above your head; then hold

70

your attention lightly there for as long as you comfortably can. Others find it more appropriate to place themselves in resonance with their heart (heart chakra); again, just let your attention focus in your heart and be aware of its love and expansiveness.

As with all meditation, however, the important thing is to stay calm, relaxed, anchored and focused. It is that paradoxical mixture of surrender and focus.

2—Earthed and anchored in our bodies

Because this meditation involves quite an intense transpersonal focus, there is a tendency for people to lose concentration, fall asleep or lift out of their bodies. The solution to this, and I advise it for all practitioners, is to be securely earthed and anchored at the beginning of the meditation.

The simplest technique for achieving this is to be aware of energy running in through the top of your head, down your spine and then down into the centre of the Earth. Another technique is to visualise yourself as a tree with deep roots. Alternatively, imagine a loop of energy from the centre of the Earth up through your waist and then back down again.

3—Tune in to problems with compassion

From our point of centre and alignment, we then let our awareness reach out beyond our immediate surroundings. We become aware of those situations and areas where there is cruelty, conflict, pain and injustice—where there is a need for love, enlightenment and healing. Let your mind travel to wherever it is drawn. It does not matter whether these situations are personal conflicts close by or events many thousands of miles away. Look at these situations with detachment and with no emotional involvement, but then be aware of them with an attitude of compassion. This compassion must, following the actual meaning of the word, be a true *passion* or *suffering with*, a deep empathy and sympathy. Again, be careful not to identify personally with the situation and do not in any way become a fellow victim. Just be aware of the circumstances with a hot love and compassion.

Compassion is a fiery love and deep vibration which seeks to heal, to save and to resurrect. To hold this compassionate attitude is crucial for it provides the launchpad and the thrust of sincerity with which we reach up to invoke energies of love, light and healing. It also provides the attitudinal fire with which we dare to call down—almost demand—these energies.

4—Pause and back to centre

We then bring our focus back to ourselves and to our centre. We pause for a little while, perhaps a minute, and prepare ourselves for the next phase of intense and disciplined work.

5—Focus on pure source and point of tension

We now lift our awareness and consciousness up to a pure source of love, light and healing energy.

The way to do this is through a very disciplined form of focus and attention. First we focus on that area a few inches above the head. (As you read this book, why not just close your eyes for a few seconds and let your focus hover at that point above your head? You will experience a distinct change of atmosphere and perhaps some sensation in the top of your skull. This is quite normal. Just be relaxed, calm and confident with it.)

Holding that focus above your head, be aware now of a pure source of energy very high above you. Be aware of that source of light and hold your focus clearly upon it. At this point we must be careful not to lose focus or let our consciousness slip away to other things. We need to hold our awareness on nothing else except that pure source high above. (If you find yourself falling asleep, drifting or lifting off, then you need to remember to earth and anchor yourself.)

To lift your attention to this source and then hold it there may require great discipline. Be aware of the need for concentration and for putting real attention into this work. It is real *work*. If we do not approach it with this awareness, then the meditation will lack focus and be ineffective.

As that high focus is held, it feels as if one is holding a real point of tension. The face and muscles around the forehead may feel strained, but this is normal and not to be a cause of concern. Be careful, though, to keep the physical body relaxed.

We feel our consciousness reaching up and then touching a peak. This peak is the source of pure energy and we now have to hold our focus and attention upon that source. There may be a temptation, through laziness or lack of discipline or a straying mind, to release this focus. Do not. The fire of our compassion should hold us up at that point of tension. In other mystical traditions this is the fiery intensity of true prayer. It is this point of tension, with the focus on high, which ensures that we are in contact with the highest possible energy fields—the closest to spirit, to God, to pure grace that we can achieve.

The holding of this point of tension will last between thirty seconds and ten minutes. It has a natural rhythm, like waves upon the ocean. When we feel the point of tension being lost—but not through laziness or lack of attention—then we just release it. Let it go. Possibly, after a short pause, you may wish to reach up again to that high focus and repeat the point of tension. This is fine, but do not do it more than three times in all. And if you do it three times you can change the quality of energy reached at each peak: first love, then light, then healing.

As the point of high focus and tension is held, be aware that energy from the source is flowing down. Your compassionate and high focus has created a bridge, or funnel, through which the energy may pass. But do not, as yet, focus on the flow downwards, because if you do, you will lose your point of tension.

6—Invocation of light, love, healing

As we feel the point of tension releasing, then we actively call down love, light and healing from the source. On behalf of all life, on behalf of all the suffering for which we felt that compassion, we invoke and demand that the energy flow.

Imagine and experience the energy flowing down. Let it keep flowing. Do not yet direct it anywhere.

After a few minutes, it becomes obvious that the flow is ending as the atmosphere and sensation change.

7—Radiation of energies

Now actively imagine or sense the energy radiating out to those situations you were aware of at the beginning of the meditation—or you can just let it be drawn magnetically to where it is needed. Be aware also that you can allow the energy to flow down and out through the whole of your body.

Be careful not to hold on to any of the energy, but to release it all. Many of us, to ensure complete distribution of all that has been invoked, end by sounding the OM. The vibration of the OM resonates in such a way as to be completely effective in releasing and distributing any remaining energy.

8—Relax

Give yourself a few minutes to relax and bring yourself back into this reality. After an intense working meditation like this you will be quite open and sensitive, so be kind and careful with yourself. Gather your energies. Be aware that your focus is back in the three-dimensional world. Sit quietly until you feel integrated and confident of your ability to cope with ordinary human social life.

The Five-Day Rhythm
Many people find it very helpful to keep to a particular invocative pattern for the five days of the full Moon, with the actual day of the full Moon providing a peak.

The two days preceding the full Moon are used for tuning in to the needs of the planet and for reaching up in our awareness and beginning the work of invocation.

The actual day of the full Moon—and its actual time—is used for intense invocation.

And the two days following the full Moon are oriented towards distributing the energy.

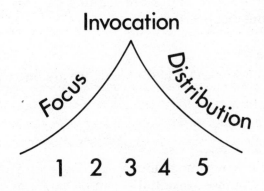

Leading a Group Full Moon Meditation—What to Say

When groups meditate at the full Moon, the structure is precisely the same as for individual meditation, except that care must be taken at the beginning for the members of the group to link together. With the complete acceptance that people should lead meditations only with words that are authentic for themselves, I nevertheless suggest the following:

Centre and align:
Let us sit quietly and each one of us in our own way come to centre and alignment.
   Pause.

Linking:
Let us link together in love and in enlightenment as a circle of service.
   Pause.

Group alignment:
We become aware of our overlighting purpose—of the group soul that overlights us.
   Pause.

We are the workers and the work. We are one with the one that is.
   Pause.

Awareness of problems:
With the fire of compassion, we become aware of world problems—those areas and situations of conflict, pain, injustice and cruelty in need of healing.
   Pause—five minutes.

Refocus:
We bring our focus back to this group.
   Gentle pause.

And we become aware again of our work and our overlighting purpose.

Gentle pause.

Focus on source:
And we become aware of a point high above us, a source of love, light and healing. With all our discipline and aspiration, we lift our consciousness up to touch that high source of spirit. And with discipline and strength, we hold that high focus.

Pause—up to five minutes.

Energy flows:
We now sense and recognise the energies of love, light and healing flowing down.

Pause—up to five minutes.

Let the energy come fully down into and through our bodies.

Gentle pause.

Distribution:
We sense and imagine this energy flowing out to where it is needed.

Pause—up to five minutes.

We release all the energy, holding on to none of it.

Pause.

Many people feel it appropriate at this point to say an invocative prayer, examples of which are given in the Appendix. Then, if it feels appropriate or you have decided to, sound the OM, either three times or in an open-ended manner.

OM.

The Annual Rhythm of the Full Moons

If we meditatively study and attune to the lunar cycle through the year, we find subtle changes of atmosphere affecting the quality of each full Moon. Each one has its own distinctive character. There are, of course, many different astrological and cosmic influences which can create that quality, but the major influence here is the sign of the zodiac that the Sun is in at the time of the full Moon. So when we talk about the Aquarius full Moon we are referring to any full Moon that occurs between January 22 and February 21; and so on.

This is so because the influential time of the full Moon lasts several days and not just a few hours; and because we live in a solar system and not a lunar system. Each full Moon then carries the atmosphere of that particular sign of the zodiac. These are the ancient Sanskrit keynotes for each sign of the Zodiac and these keynotes can be used as seed thoughts for meditation:

Aries: I come forth and from the plane of mind I rule.
Taurus: I see and when the eye is open all is light.
Gemini: I recognise my other self and in the waning of that self, I grow and glow.
Cancer: I build a lighted house and therein dwell.
Leo: I am That and That I am.
Virgo: I am the Mother and the child. I, God, I, matter, am.
Libra: I choose the way which leads between the two great lines of force.
Scorpio: Warrior I am and from the battle I emerge triumphant.
Sagittarius: I see the goal. I reach that goal and then I see another.
Capricorn: Lost am I in light supernal, yet on that light I turn my back.
Aquarius: Water of life am I poured forth for thirsty men.
Pisces: I leave my father's home, and turning back, I save.

78

Each of these keynotes expresses the particular zodiacal lesson for each full Moon. It provides a key, as does all true astrology, to the challenges and solutions that we meet on our evolutionary path. Each full Moon, then, represents an opportunity to focus upon and learn about that particular sign of the zodiac, and actually to experience its insights and energy. If this meditational focus is held over several years, it can provide a profound and intuitive way to learn astrology which I, to my surprise, once experienced. For several years, I led group full Moon meditations in Glastonbury. It was never a huge group, but I began each evening with a short talk to attune the group to the quality of that particular full Moon. I always prepared carefully, with some study and contemplative meditation, and gave passable introductions. After leading these meditations for three years, I glanced one day at a friend's birth chart, never having studied astrology. The information jumped out at me as I instinctively understood the chart's pattern and energies. I was astonished that I could read it. Three years of attuning to each zodiacal constellation at the full Moon had taken my psyche into the beginnings of a natural astrological wisdom.

Many who work with the full Moons also recognise a specific annual rhythm in which three of the full Moons are particularly potent for invocative work. These are the full Moons in April, May and June—in Aries, Taurus and Gemini.

The Living Legend of Wesak

The Taurus full Moon is also known as the Festival of Wesak and is recognised in the East as the Buddha's birthday. It is felt by many people to be the spiritual high point of the year. According to esoteric teachings, during Wesak all the illuminated beings and true spiritual teachers cooperate to invoke a great annual blessing for the Earth. There is a beautiful living legend, described in detail by C.W. Leadbeater, Alice Bailey and many others, of a ceremony which takes place in the Himalayas at Wesak. Perfectly integrated and liberated human beings, free of karma and the need to incarnate—our true spiritual teachers and gurus—congregate in this valley. Using dancing patterns and sound, they work an intense invocative meditation. The actual invocation is then focused and received by the Christ working with the Buddha. Whether one fully believes the story or not, it has a mythic quality that speaks directly to the heart.

There is a valley, lying at a rather high altitude in the foothills of the Himalayan-Tibet ranges. It is surrounded by high mountains on all sides except towards the northeast, where there is a narrow opening in the mountain ranges. The valley is, therefore, bottle-shaped in contour, with the neck of the bottle to the northeast, and it widens very considerably towards the south. Up towards the northern end, close to the neck of the bottle, there is to be found a huge flat rock. There are no trees or shrubs in the valley, which is covered with a kind of coarse grass, but the sides of the mountains are covered with trees.

At the time of the full Moon of Taurus, pilgrims from all the surrounding districts begin to gather; the holy men and lamas find their way into the valley and fill the southern and middle parts, leaving the northeastern end relatively free. There, so the legend runs, there gathers a group of those great Beings Who are the Custodians on Earth of God's Plan for our planet and for humanity . . . . The esotericists of the world may call Them the Masters of the Wisdom, the planetary Hierarchy . . . . Or we can call them the Rishis of the Hindu scriptures, or the Society of Illumined Minds . . . . They are the Great Intuitives and the Great Companions who with Their wisdom, love and knowledge, stand as a protective wall around our race, and seek to lead us on, step by step (as They Themselves were led in Their time) from darkness to light, from the unreal to the real, and from death to immortality. This group of knowers of divinity are the main participants in the Wesak Festival. They range Themselves in the northeastern end of the valley and in concentric circles prepare Themselves for a great act of service . . . .

As the hour of the full Moon approaches, a stillness settles down upon the crowd, and all look towards the northeast. Certain ritualistic movements take place, in which the grouped Masters and Their disciples of all ranks take up symbolic positions, and form on the floor of the valley such significant symbols as the five-pointed star, with the Christ standing at the highest point; or a triangle, with the Christ at the apex; or a cross, and other well known formations, all of which have a deep and potent meaning. This is all done to the sound of certain chanted words and esoteric phrases. The expectancy in the waiting, onlooking crowds becomes very great, and the tension is real and increasing. Through the entire body of people there seems to be felt a stimulation or potent vibration which has the effect of awakening the souls of those present, fusing and blending the group into one united whole, and lifting all into a great act of spiritual demand, readiness, and expectancy . . . .

The chanting and the rhythmic weaving grows stronger, and all the participants and the watching crowd raise their eyes towards the sky in the direction of the narrow part of the valley. Just a few minutes before the exact time of the full moon, in the far distance, a tiny speck can be seen in the sky. It comes nearer and nearer, and grows in clarity and definiteness of outline, until the form of the Buddha can be seen, seated in the cross-legged position, clad in His saffron coloured robe, bathed in light and colour, and with His hand extended in Blessing. When He arrives at the point exactly over the great rock, hovering there in the air over the heads of the three great Lords, a great mantram, used only once a year, at the Festival, is intoned by the Christ, and the entire group of people in the valley fall upon their faces. This invocation sets up a great vibration or thought current which is of such potency that it reaches up from the group of aspirants, disciples or initiates who employ it, to God Himself. It marks the supreme moment of intensive spiritual effort throughout the year, and the spiritual vitalisation of humanity and the spiritual effects last throughout the succeeding months. The effect of the Great Invocation is universal or cosmic, and serves to link us up with that cosmic centre of spiritual force from which all created beings have come. The blessing is poured forth, and the Christ—as the Representative of humanity—receives it in trust, for distribution.

Thus, so the legend runs, the Buddha returns once a year to bless the world, transmitting through the Christ renewed spiritual life. Slowly then the Buddha recedes into the distance, until again only a faint speck can be seen in the sky, and this eventually disappears. The whole ceremonial blessing, from the time of the first appearance in the distance until the moment the Buddha fades out of view, takes just eight minutes. The Buddha's annual sacrifice for humanity (for He comes back only at great cost) is over, and He returns again to that high place where He works and waits. Year after year He comes back in blessing; year after year the same ceremony takes place. Year after year He and His great Brother, the Christ, work in closest cooperation for the spiritual benefit of humanity.

(From *The Wesak Festival*, a booklet published by the Lucis Trust)

With the Taurus full Moon as the invocative peak, the Aries full Moon before it holds a general note of compassion and of tuning in to the planet's problems; it is called by some people the Christ Festival. The Gemini full Moon then continues the focus on invocation with a particular awareness of distributing and radiating the energy; some people call the Gemini full Moon, World Invocation Day.

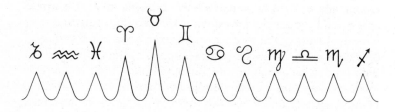

The Lunar Cycle and Personal Transformation

One great beauty of our emerging culture is the growing recognition of the deep relationship between psychological and spiritual change. In many ways people are experiencing intimate similarities between psychotherapeutic change and spiritual transformation. Therapists are becoming spiritual counsellors and spiritual counsellors are becoming therapists. This is happening because of the similarity between certain psychotherapeutic techniques and certain spiritual exercises. The similarity of these techniques and exercises lies in various areas: in creative self-reflection; in entering into active dialogue with the various conscious and subconscious aspects of the psyche; in listening to the Self; and in allowing transformational attitudes and energies, such as forgiveness and grace, to enter the psyche and to heal. The lunar cycle can be used as a rhythm to help transformation.

The basic rhythm is very straightforward. When the Moon is dark: contemplation, reflection, achieving clarity. When the Moon is light: action, transformation.

When the Moon is dark, the atmosphere is extremely helpful for careful self-analysis and examination. It is the best time to think about problems that require clarity, both within ourselves and in the outer world.

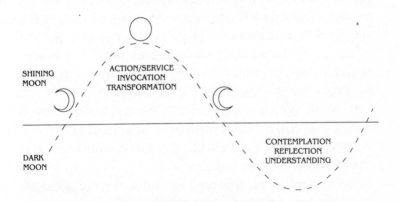

SHINING MOON

ACTION/SERVICE
INVOCATION
TRANSFORMATION

DARK MOON

CONTEMPLATION
REFLECTION
UNDERSTANDING

As the first thin crescent of the new Moon appears, it signals that we can begin to shift our orientation. From a period of deep and reflective contemplation, we begin to move into a less introspective, more dynamic and more expansive attitude. We become aware of the incredible energy and dynamism of spirit as it works through us and through all creation. We move into a time of creative spiritual action and purposefulness, a period when we can be of greatest spiritual service.

At the full Moon the atmosphere is really conducive to pushing ourselves through an expansion of consciousness or breaking deeply ingrained patterns to move into a new attitude.

The basic rhythm for effecting this kind of work is always the same. During the dark side of the Moon we contemplate what it is that we want to change or to achieve. For example, we might have a pattern of disempowerment when confronted with authority figures; or we might be short-tempered with our partner; or we know that it is time generally to adopt a more loving, more creative, more thoughtful attitude. While the Moon is dark, we think about the change we want to make and look at it from all angles. We come to a clear understanding of what we want to do and a clear understanding of how the change will affect us. This process of thoughtful contemplation produces a clear idea, a *model*, of how we will be when the change is complete. It is helpful to put this model into words, so that we have an affirmation with which to work. The affirmation is always stated in the present: I *am* loving and thoughtful. It is said as if the change were already completed.

All of this work is done in meditation and in silent reflection. It is a form of *active* meditation in which, in complete privacy, we act as our own therapist and counsellor, in tandem with our soul or higher self.

At first sight of the new crescent Moon, we make certain that our seed thought is clear and, instead of just contemplating it, we begin to work with and actually to experience the energy of the seed thought.

As the full Moon approaches we build up our focus of inner activity, bringing the new model of ourselves into full manifestation at the actual time of the full Moon. At the full Moon, with clear spiritual will, we fully experience the new model within our meditation and we totally commit ourselves to manifesting the change in real life.

When the full Moon has passed, we then relax our focus. And we look to see to what degree we have actually manifested the change. If we find that we have not done so well, then we simply contemplate the whole business again and, if appropriate, try once more at the next full Moon.

Now, this is an extremely useful, practical and beautiful rhythm, and if people would only adopt it into their private spiritual practice it would provide them with a framework that is disciplined, creative and empowering for their future—whatever other chaos or pain or illusion is in their lives. It provides a clear, safe and understandable way of passing through time, through transformational process and through change.

I would like to illustrate this method with a personal story. Some years ago I spent a lot of time with a very young child who badly irritated me. In my experience the infant was suffocatingly clingy and I reacted very badly to the child's touch, but this child liked me and was always wanting to climb and sit on me. It drove me crazy. I spent months analysing the child and analysing my reaction. I looked at my own childhood and parenting. I used all the methods from my own psychotherapeutic experience and training. I had some insights, but none which changed my attitude. Finally I decided that I could not carry on being psychological and philosophical. I had to change. The situation was simple: Here was a child who needed loving. I could no longer delay what I had to do—both for the child and for my own integrity. I had to actively love the child—nothing else.

I decided, therefore, that I must by an act of will simply change my response and reaction to the child—from irritation to one of active love. During the period when the Moon was dark I made my decision and began to contemplate what it would be like in the changed situation. In my meditation I began to create a model of myself, changed. I loved the child climbing on me and clinging to me. I invited the infant, in my meditation, to do it. I could experience myself actively loving the infant.

When the new crescent Moon appeared, I began to gear up for the change, putting my personal spiritual will-power fully behind the change. Approaching the full Moon I went into the mode of general ecological awareness, compassion and invocation in order to do my usual monthly inner work. It is very important, in pushing for these personal changes, to put the regular spiritual work and focus first. The personal change comes second, its effectiveness occurring in the grace of dedicated service.

As I kept to my normal full Moon work of awareness and invocation, I simultaneously held clearly in my awareness my relationship with the child, my needed transformation and my model. At the time of the full Moon I willed myself to experience that I had changed and that I fully loved the infant, actively encouraging the child to be on me. I made the model I had created fully incarnate into me and I willed my experience of fully loving the child into my whole psyche, into my whole body. I then relaxed the inner work and focused on dealing with the three-dimensional 'real life' child.

The infant approached and clambered on to me. I smiled and I cuddled. It felt good. I could love. My pattern was broken. (Months later I realised that my reaction had been based in a fear and jealousy of the child's vulnerability. The child was behaving the way that I wanted to, but did not dare.)

Be careful, though, when using this technique not to repress shadow aspects which will only surface in another form. Be therapeutically aware of yourself and careful and loving to yourself. Nevertheless what I am suggesting is that sometimes we need just to get on with the business of changing and loving and, by an act of will, simply do it.

Be careful also only to use this technique when you are fully aware of what you are doing and are doing it fully in alignment with your inner self and its unfoldment to a greater expression of wisdom, enlightenment and love.

This way of working with the full Moon can also be adapted to achieving an expansion of consciousness. There may, for instance, be a quality of spirit or a new awareness of which we have caught a subtle hint and we want to experience it more fully. It is, however, a strain to do so. Using the Moon's rhythm and our personal will we can glide into a fuller experience of the new consciousness. Again, while the Moon is dark we contemplate and come to a clear understanding of what we are seeking to achieve and we then will ourselves into it, peaking our effort at the full Moon.

We need to be absolutely clear, though, that the energy that fuels the change comes from our sincerity in doing the compassionate invocative meditation for our environment. The service must come first. There is nothing selfish and egocentric then in using that rhythm for our own spiritual transformation—for that, too, in its ripple, radiant and holographic effect, is of immense service to our environment and relationships.

To recap the procedure:

1: The dark side of the Moon is used to contemplate and fully understand the change. We create a scenario and experience—a model—of how we will be when changed.

2: At the crescent of the new Moon, we gear up for the work. We complete the model and begin to try it on for size.

3: As the full Moon approaches, we fill the model with intention, purpose and will, and a perfect expectation of its completion.

4: Over the three days of the full Moon, we bring the model into full experience. We bring it into cellular incarnation. We express in the present, in the now, that we are changed. And, most importantly, we actually have the self-discipline to behave in a better way. *We act differently.*

5: We then relax and let the spiritual dust settle. We observe how we have changed.

As a final word I would only add that for really major transformations, one may need to contemplate them for several months in advance. We can then use Wesak as the time of transformation.

New Moon Dancing

As part of the lunar rhythm the group with which I work always meets at the new Moon for sacred dance, ceremony and an informal sharing. We find it a very useful and enjoyable evening, providing us with a bridge out of the more contemplative phase of the inner work into the more active attitude.

7
The Solstices, Equinoxes & Fire Festivals Introduction

Changing Cultures

In the opening chapter I suggested that as spirit is in a process of continual revelation, no religious forms can be considered permanent. To think that any particular belief or ceremony—no matter how dear or sacramental—is a fixed piece of our sacred environment is to misunderstand the nature of time and change. It also misunderstands the relativity of human culture and how we human beings interpret our environment and reality. Culture and our interpretations of life are always changing.

Just as spirit is in a continuous process of revelation, so humanity is continually re-creating and reformulating the way in which it understands reality. The sociologist Emile Durkheim suggested long ago that religion and deity were, in fact, ways in which society worshipped itself. He pointed out how our ideas of God and our religious structures reflect the culture in which we live. In a patriarchal society, for example, we have a patriarchal God—patriarchal men worship themselves. Durkheim's perception was cutting and insightful. Indeed there have been many different religious forms and all these, in one way or another, have reflected the culture in which they appeared.

Recently I was looking at comments by European and American academics that politics in Africa had distinct religious elements. This was particularly observed in the tribal dancing and chants that occurred at political meetings, and also in the charismatic performance of political leaders who resembled medicine men and shamans. Looking around my own society, I noticed then the startling resemblance between Western public political meetings and church services. There everyone is, sitting in rows facing one person who is the focus of attention and giving some kind of oration. This does not necessarily mean that the political meeting and the religious meeting are doing the same thing—although, to a startling degree, they display a similar structure. The similarity is due to the fact that both happenings emerge from the same culture.

I mention all this to underline the fact that religious and spiritual beliefs and festivals are truly coloured and created by the culture from which they emerge. Indeed, completely materialistic social theorists and anthropologists would say that all metaphysical and mystical activities are cultural and social rituals in which men and women—in order to gain psychological security and social stability—pretend to have some control over circumstances which in fact are uncontrollable.

All of these thoughts are extremely relevant to the Solar and Fire festivals.

The New Awareness
We are at the very beginning of re-creating our celebration and experience of these festivals. The new way of working with the lunar cycle already has a certain innate clarity; this is due to the fact that it is concerned, to a degree, with a pure form of inner work that is not affected by social and cultural dynamics. The Solar and Fire festivals, however, are a direct manifestation of humanity's relationship with its ecological environment: earthly, solar and cosmic. These festivals emerge from human culture and its awareness of natural and spiritual ecology.

The Solar festivals—the Equinoxes and Solstices—are concerned with the relationship of the Earth with the Sun and with the instinctive, mystical and philosophical issues which are inspired by this relationship.

The Fire festivals on the other hand—known in the Celtic tradition as Imbolc, Beltane, Lammas and Samhain—are concerned with the passage of the seasons, with horticulture, with nature and with the fairy and angelic realms.

The problem we face in working with these festivals is that humanity is currently in the process of completely redefining its relationship with its ecological environment. In fact, this particular problem—that of a changing relationship between humanity and its environment—has been with us from the time of the very first civilisations. As we have become agriculturally and technologically efficient and as our societies have become more and more complex, so we have grown increasingly distant, psychologically and physically, from our natural and cosmic environment.

This psychological distance, in which we do not perceive how our lives affect and are affected by the environment, has resulted in the present ecological crisis. It has also led us into a way of thinking in which we do not recognise the stark realities. In 'primitive' society it is only too obvious how vulnerable we are to elemental forces. In a pastoral or rural society, it is again only too obvious how our lives are intertwined with the passage of the seasons and the natural cycles of growth. In contemporary society, as many thousands of writers and commentators have lamented, we have no contact with these natural realities. We no longer acknowledge the fact that Gaia and solar energy provide *all* our nurture and provision. We have lost touch with these realities to such an extent that we have created some societies of mass surplus and mass greed, and others which suffer and endure mass need. We have lost all sense of what is natural, including our sense of natural justice.

In contemporary culture it appears that we have no need to recognise how crucial these natural relationships are. We are in a state of mass denial; we do not acknowledge these relationships and we certainly do not honour them. Modern world religions have conspired in this denial. They celebrate inspiring cultural ideologies, but only with rare exceptions do they bother to honour the realities of the sacred space in which we live. Worse than that, contemporary world religions positively frown upon those belief systems which honour the invisible realities, judging them pagan, primitive and superstitious.

And if the modern world religions have no time for a spiritual ecology, then mainstream culture and the mainstream intelligentsia have even less time for it. At the very least, mainstream intelligentsia patronisingly judges a 'pagan' attitude as harmless romanticism; at the very worst it judges it with a harsh and almost fascist arrogance. But times are changing. Vegetarianism and ecological awareness were both once considered cranky, but are now mainstream. The new awareness of spiritual ecology will, I dare to guess, also shortly be mainstream and the current harsh judgements upon it will be seen to be religious and intellectual narrow-mindedness.

There are some groups, of course, who do still celebrate the Solar and Fire festivals according to ancient traditions and their work is to be honoured. I am thinking especially of the Druids, and of the Wiccan and the Native American traditions. How these groups work can be a very useful inspiration.

What we face, then, is a stimulating challenge. The challenge is to create festivals which relate to our sacred ecological realities and which also relate to our special and local communities; festivals which have a cosmic and sacred perspective, but which are based in our immediate environment. Our goal is to find ways of honouring and celebrating our crucial environmental relationships. We need to do this in our cities as well as in sacred places in the landscape.

My strong feeling is that, unlike the clear structure of the group meditations at the full Moon, there will be no standard format for celebrating the Equinoxes, Solstices and Fire festivals. There will be similar themes for meditation and reflection, but how groups *celebrate* them will vary from locality to locality. Not only this but the actual timing of the Fire festivals will also differ according to local ecological conditions. Preparation, planting and harvesting, and the angelic rhythm of cooperation all occur at different times in different places.

What I want to provide in the following few pages is a general understanding of the festivals and an attempt at an overview of what the general trends and structures for their celebration might be.

8
Solstices & Equinoxes

Basic Information

First, in case there is any confusion, let us be clear:

The Solstices are the two points of the year when the Sun reaches its greatest declination in relation to the Earth, north or south. The Winter Solstice marks the shortest day of the year north of the equator and occurs about December 21. The Summer Solstice marks the longest day of the year north of the equator and occurs about June 21.

The Equinoxes are the two moments in the year when the Sun is exactly above the equator and, at the equator, day and night are of equal length. They also mark the points where the Sun's annual pathway and the celestial equator intersect. The Spring Equinox thus marks the half-way point between the Summer and Winter Solstices and occurs about March 21. The Autumn Equinox marks the half-way point between the Summer and Winter Solstices and occurs about September 21.

Let us now draw together the various threads that give the Solar festivals their influence. To begin, let us imagine ourselves in that social and ecological situation which existed many thousands of years ago, before even the first great river basin civilisations. Imagine ourselves in that state which some call 'primitive'—an insult to some and flattering to others. We are living directly off the earth, no farmer, no cultivator, mediating between us and our survival. We are prey to certain dangers and all the time we are closely watching our environment. At night, even with the Moon, there is danger. With the rising of the fiery orb at dawn comes light, comes safety and comes heat. Then, as the day nears its end, as the Sun begins to disappear, we need again to prepare for the dark of the night. There are two existences: that of the day, that of the night.

And what assurance is there that the Sun will rise the next morning, that darkness will turn to light?

What else do we notice as a tribal people with no urban or industrial culture? We observe the passing of the seasons and the lengthening and then shortening of the days. The position and angle of the Sun in the sky changes. At one point in the year, the Sun passes almost directly over us and at this time there also occurs the longest day. At another point in the year the Sun is low on the horizon and we have the shortest day. As the days get colder so the Sun gives us less of its time. Again, there is the question: how do we know, as the days shorten and the nights lengthen, that the Sun will not forsake us completely? There is no guarantee that Winter will give way to Spring. What is there reliably to bind this fiery deity to our existence?

We can only trust. We must have faith.

More than simple faith, however, we can address the Sun as a god, as perhaps the Greatest Deity, recognising its power, its saving presence and calling on it to be faithful in its relationship with us. The Sun is the source of light, heat, safety—yet the Sun is always moving, appearing and disappearing. It is only sensible, then, that we attempt to form a relationship with this great being and that we do what we can—prayer, ritual, offerings, sacrifice—to keep the Sun faithful in its relationship with us.

Subtler Realities

But there is another way to view how the Sun intertwines with these understandable physical anxieties. This way is that of the shamans and those who contemplate occult realities. This is a more subtle knowledge which concerns the true relationship of the Sun with the Earth.

Magnetically, the Earth is held by the Sun's energy field, the Sun being the Earth's parent. More than that, the very life-force of all existence on Earth has its source in the life-force of the Sun. The prana of the Sun is the prana of all life on Earth. (*Prana*—Sanskrit word commonly used by Western practitioners of holistic health, meaning the invisible energy which provides the dynamism and force of manifest life.) Life as we know it on this planet is completely dependent upon the energy of the Sun. This is both a scientific and an occult reality. Through photosynthesis plant life converts the Sun's light into digestible energy forms for our bodies. Occultly, the pranic dynamism of the Sun sustains the very life-force of our bodies.

At a purely pragmatic and materialist level, then, we have the intense practical importance of the Sun. No Sun equals no life as we know it on Earth. It is hardly surprising that the Sun has been so central to religious forms in the past.

"To primitive peoples the Sun was the innate Fire of bodies, the Fire of Nature, the Author of Life, heat, and ignition. He was to them the efficient cause of all generation, for without him there was no movement, no existence, no form. He was to them immense, indivisible, imperishable and everywhere present. It was their need of light, and of his creative energy, that was felt by all men; and nothing was more fearful to them than his absence. His beneficent influences caused his identification with the Principle of Good. And the *Brahma* of the Hindus, and *Mithras* of the Persians, and *Athom, Amun, Phtha* and *Osiris* of the Egyptians, the *Bel* of the Chaldeans, the *Adonai* of the Phoenicians, the *Adonis* and *Apollo* of the Greeks, became but personifications of the Sun, the regenerating Principle, image of that fecundity which perpetuates and rejuvenates the world's existence." (Albert Pike, *Morals and Dogma*.)

But, some people may ask, why celebrate and honour the Sun? We don't worship our washing machines or power stations. The fact that the Sun is central to our lives is important, but so what? It is millions of miles away and we cannot do anything about it. It is a great swirling fiery energy, one of millions of similar stars; and we are just an insignificant life-force on an insignificant planet. Why give it anything but scientific attention?

Again, the accusation here is the sociological one that we are psychologically insecure, superstitious and attempting to control something that is uncontrollable.

Are We Being Superstitious?

There are two answers to this accusation of superstition.

The first answer concerns the very nature of celebration. The second answer concerns the inner nature of the Sun.

Celebration

It is not superstitious to celebrate a friend's birthday. Equally, it is not superstitious to celebrate the passage of time and of the seasons.

For all the woes and miseries of human existence, our species has always recognised events that require celebrating and enjoyed a good party. Partying and celebration are something that we do well. We may do other things terribly and with cruelty and selfishness, but we know instinctively how to party. For some people any event will be taken as an opportunity to celebrate. In my experience people within the emerging spiritual culture, almost without exception, welcome the joy, fun, amusement, relief, release and healing of a good party. I do not want to make any blanket judgements, but beware of yourself if you become that spiritual type aloof to human enjoyment. Spirit seeks to incarnate fully through our creaturehood and the happiness of dance and celebration deeply helps that process.

At one level, therefore, I do not think we should care about this accusation of superstition. There is a part of me that shouts back: "So what if I am superstitious? You, the accuser, are just a materialistic kill-joy. Come and dance. Stop criticising."

It is part of a natural human existence to celebrate the passage of time, to celebrate important signals as time passes. This natural exuberance should not be repressed or feared, but released to create festivals and great parties. It is also part of our existence to fete those whom we love and honour and I experience no embarrassment in loving the Sun. I am not saying that the Sun is God or that the Sun is All That Is. I am, however, acknowledging that the Sun is an extraordinary being and certainly *a* god in our cosmos. To deny that is to ignore reality. To celebrate the Sun is part of the richness of our lives.

The Inner Being of the Sun

We can also, I believe, declare that it is not superstitious to give the Sun a personality. It is a dull and unimaginative world if we do not relate to the Sun as a being. We commune with trees. We recognise the presence of a great mountain. We are beginning to understand the being who is Gaia. Many of us increasingly recognise that all life forms, of whatever realm or kingdom, possess consciousness. Recognising this we can hardly ignore that extraordinary life form who is the Sun. It is surely worth contemplating its consciousness.

Many meditators and mystics, in their silence, contemplate and investigate the Sun. They let their awareness explore its energy, essence and consciousness. Imagine letting your mind enter into the Sun. In doing this, mystic workers come into a completely new and transcendent understanding.

The great Paracelsus wrote:

"There is an earthly Sun, which is the cause of all heat, and all who are able to see may see the Sun; and those who are blind and cannot see him may feel his heat. There is an Eternal Sun, which is the source of all wisdom, and those whose spiritual senses have awakened to life will see that Sun and be conscious of His existence; but those who have not attained spiritual consciousness may yet feel His power by an inner faculty which is called intuition."

The secret suggested here is that the Sun is a spiritual being in the same way that we are spiritual beings. We have an ephemeral social and psychological personality—an outer self. We also have an inner, multi-dimensional and higher self—our soul. When in the classic Hindu form we hold our hands in a prayerful position and bow as we meet another human being, saying, "Namaskara," we deliberately greet the soul of our friend. We ignore the outer shell of physical body and transient personality, and we affirm our relationship with that person's essence.

In the quotation from Paracelsus above, we read about acknowledging the inner essence of the Sun. We ignore its fiery vehicle for that, like our bodies, is temporary and we attune to its real essence and being. This is, in fact, a classic exercise of occult meditation: to sit, attuned, centred and in silence, and contemplate the inner being of the Sun. The oldest recorded prayer, the Sanskrit *The Gayatri*, is precisely an attunement to and evocation of the Sun:

The Gayatri
O Thou who givest sustenance to the Universe,
From Whom all things proceed,
And to Whom all things return,
Unveil to us the face of the true Spiritual Sun,
Hidden by a disc of golden light,
That we may know the truth,
And do our whole duty
As we journey to Thy Sacred Feet.

In my own meditations for many years I have attuned to the inner being of the Sun. I cannot do it unless I am perfectly still and earthed in my meditation; even then I do not always glide easily into the attunement. I begin by becoming fully aware of the light and the heat and of how close the Sun is to us. I do not take the light and heat for granted; I truly recognise its source and its significance. I become aware of how our planet is held in orbit by the Sun's gravity and how we are indeed just a part of the solar system.

This awareness—recognising and greeting the closeness of the Sun—is sufficient to lift me out of my usual personality and materialistic focus as I begin to appreciate my real cosmic environment. Fully aware of the Sun's presence, I then release my consciousness and focus to become aware of the inner being of the Sun. I need to continue to hold myself perfectly still and anchored, because with the new awareness and energy there is a temptation to get caught up in the thrill and excitement of the experience; and this causes my consciousness to lift off out of my body and I lose my centre. So I hold myself still and carefully anchored and release myself to this new awareness.

The experience then is that my consciousness has moved into a completely transpersonal and cosmic realm. I experience totally new qualities of light, of life and of love. I let this new awareness settle in my consciousness and my mind, and I then deliberately share the experience with the rest of my body, bringing the awareness and sensation down through my chakras; I then let it tingle through every cell of my body. Finally, I radiate it outwards through my body and I let myself glow as an ecologically useful radiation into my environment. I hold this radiation for as long as feels appropriate, anything between ten seconds and five minutes.

I am always inspired and deeply touched by this experience. It places many things in perspective for me and strengthens me in my attempt continuously to greet the soul in all beings—but particularly to greet the soul and inner life of the cosmos. This is a way of exploring cosmic consciousness, of exploring what that word 'God' really means.

The Mythical Lessons of Solar Death and Rebirth

I wrote briefly above about the Sun's apparent death and rebirth happening on both a daily and an annual basis: day into night into day, Summer into Winter into Summer. This is its natural rhythm and surely for us to celebrate as we acknowledge our relationship with this magnificent glowing orb and how this relationship marks our passage through time together.

There is, however, a more subtle understanding of this passage and a deeper symbolic interpretation. This interpretation, revolving around death and rebirth, formed the basis for the central ritual of many of the mystery traditions and is still to be found in contemporary Masonic ceremonies.

In the past, contemplative philosophers of occult realities perceived the profound affinity between the story of the Sun's annual death and rebirth and the story of the human soul's descent into and then out of incarnation.

According to esoteric spiritual philosophy, human life is the manifestation of a divine spark or soul deliberately taking on human form. Each of us is an eternal inner being who has intentionally incarnated into the energy-matter of the human personality—physical, etheric, emotional, mental energy-matter. The intrinsic vibration or quality of the inner being is 'love'. (Let us, for the sake of ease, call it 'love'. We mean a love, though, that is cosmic, wise and enlightened—not sentimental.) The vibration or quality of the human vehicle and personality, however, is something other than love. The purpose, then, of this deliberate incarnation of the inner being, or soul, is to change the vibration and quality of the human personality into love.

According to this view, and particularly in the interpretation of the mystery religions, the soul 'sacrifices' itself into incarnation. The soul figuratively dies or descends into the underworld of the personality; or the soul is cut into many pieces (a metaphor for many incarnations) and scattered across the globe. Only after a long period of time, after struggles and heroic mythical deeds, does the soul resurrect. It has completed its allotted task and has finally brought its incarnational personality fully into the vibration of love. The personality and the inner being now share the same quality and vibration; the work of raising dross matter into gold is complete. And the inner being is released from further incarnations on the great wheel of human karma, of death and rebirth.

Contemplating the rhythm of the Sun, esoteric philosophers saw the symbolic similarity between its voyage and that of the human soul. The Sun lives so that we may live. It dies at the Winter Solstice only to resurrect, to reach a peak of dynamic life at the Summer Solstice and then to begin to die again.

Death and resurrection. Incarnation, reincarnation. The great rhythms.

Even more deeply—working with the spiritual laws of correspondence and with the mystical idea that human life microcosmically reflected the realities of macrocosmic life —it was thought that this rhythm of sacrifice illustrated the way in which Deity itself created all life. This profound philosophical idea stated that all life is the manifestation of the sacrifice of Deity Itself. The very soul of all existence is Deity descended into matter.

The Cosmic Drama

Three threads intertwine here, all of them telling the same story, but each at a very different level. *The story is of the willing sacrifice of a higher consciousness to create the soul and to be the dynamic essence of a less evolved and smaller consciousness.* The three levels are those of

i. The human soul incarnating for the human personality
ii. The Sun incarnating for the Earth
iii. The Supreme Deity incarnating for all existence.

Here we have the source of the great mystery religions,

the myths of the slaying then resurrection of the Sun Deities and the great solar cults. Here we have Osiris slain. Here we have the crucifixion of the Cosmic Christ upon the equal-armed cross of matter. Here we have the story of the purpose of each human soul and the story of all spirit.

The Inner Dynamics of Ceremony

The religions and festivals associated with the solar cycle now take on deep and almost bewildering significance, for in them we can find a contemplation of the meaning of life. Great and sacred mystery rituals were performed in honour of the solar cycle. Within these sacred dramas, the celebrants in their clothes, actions and words represented the various aspects of the divine story. A central theme of many of them was a symbolic death and resurrection of new members of the cult, a feature that was corruptly and mistakenly adapted in some cultures to include actual human sacrifice. Some of these sacred dramas were part of public festivals and some of them were restricted only to the initiated members of the mystery religion or esoteric school.

A deeper dimension was added to these solar celebrations by an occult knowledge of the inner dynamics of ceremony. There were two particular dynamics at work.

First, in praising, honouring and invoking the blessing of the Solar Deity, the celebrants with a shamanistic awareness recognised that they were genuinely invoking a greater flow of the Sun's prana and other beneficent energies. Temples for these ceremonies were specifically located on ley lines and at significant points on the Earth's surface. At these places—similar to acupuncture points on the meridians of the human body—the natural vortex of Earth energy enhanced the invoked energy and amplified its radiation over the surrounding landscape. The ceremonies were not only of spiritual significance for the individuals involved, but also produced great blessings for the environment which, in turn, manifested in greater fertility and more plentiful harvests. These ceremonies were part of a deep and sacred ecological awareness.

Second, it was recognised that when people act out cosmic principles they actually attract unto themselves the energy of those principles. This is based in the simple law that 'like attracts like'. (For example, theatrically act like Mars, dressed in red and brandishing a piece of iron that holds the symbol of Mars—and you will begin to attract and channel Mars energy.) In a ritual, therefore, where celebrants actively represent cosmic principles of birth, creation and death, the temple in which it takes place begins to glow with cosmic energy. The cosmic principles themselves respond to their microcosmic representatives. This amplified prana, this enhanced spiritual energy, radiates to give a blessing to the surrounding area, again enhancing and increasing the fertility of the local ecology.

Many Approaches to the Solstices and Equinoxes

By now we are beginning to appreciate the multi-dimensionality of the Solar festivals. There are several different ways of celebrating the Solstices and Equinoxes. It is helpful to list them.

1. The recognition and celebration of the passage of time.

2. 'Superstitious' ceremonies which ask the Sun to remain faithful to us and not go away.

3. Festivals which celebrate the external and obvious importance of the Sun, and its crucial role in sustaining life on Earth.

4. Festivals which are more shamanistically aware and use the Solstices and Equinoxes as signals to celebrate and invoke a flow of solar prana and blessing for the environment.

5. Deeper celebrations which contemplate the inner essence of the Sun and the greater cosmic mysteries.

6. Rituals which symbolically reflect the inner realities of incarnation, death and resurrection—human, solar and cosmic.

So where does all this leave us? How are we to celebrate these festivals? As I wrote earlier, we are in the very early days of the emergence of a new culture and I do not, therefore, believe that I can lay down any clear formulae. There are, however, a few pointers.

Private Celebration

The first element in private celebration of these festivals is to take them seriously. We need to give them thoughtful time and some intelligent contemplation. We need to have a *relationship* with them and relationships result only if there is an investment of personal energy and attention.

In my experience the most important understandings of these festivals come first through a silent contemplation of them. These festivals say meaningful things in silence. They give us insights about ourselves, about the passage of time, about the life around us and about sacred realities. The fact that we know where we are located in the cosmos can bring us a deep satisfaction. Our creaturehood, perhaps threatened by life in a city or on this dangerous twentieth-century planet, finds a distinct safety in knowing where it is in space and time.

So we need to meditate with them.

When Galileo pointed out that the Earth revolves around the Sun, and not vice versa, he was accused by the Roman Church of heresy. Intellectually, he is no longer accused of this crime. But there is a different cultural heresy in the fact that we do not, within our consciousness, recognise that it *is* the Earth which is spinning and that we do, in fact, revolve around the Sun. We intellectually know about our location, but we do not *realise* it. People do not know where they are! How can we have any sense of peace or knowledge of our place in the scheme of things if we do not know where we are?

And do we really notice the passage of time? We celebrate our birthdays and other mainstream cultural events. We notice the aging process and we notice history, but we miss the point. As time passes, we have no control over the process. We have no choice but to pass through time and as we do so the only certain fact is that things change and transform. Time is the dimension of transformation. Time is a manifestation of cosmic purpose. Cosmic consciousness would have us change and we experience this transformation through the dimension of time. Remove time and . . . .

At a certain level of our being, as we change from being personalities tied to the images and rhythms of Western commercial existence, as we begin to search for our true identity and as we locate ourselves—here on Earth, revolving around the Sun, within this cosmos, passing through time, all this being the reality of where we are located—we can find a certain peace. Knowing where we are brings this peace, but it is not a peace that keeps the mind quiet or gives ecstasy to our consciousness. It is a peace in the body and in the cells of our being. It brings us into incarnation and we *accept* where we are.

When the Moon is dark and we are in the rhythm of contemplative meditation, it is the perfect time to study the consciousness-expanding, love-inspiring mysteries of our relationship with the Sun, cosmos and time. Then, at the Solstices and Equinoxes, we open ourselves to the inner impulse and atmosphere of that moment; we surrender to inspiration. At the same time we make the effort to put ourselves into active relationship with the Sun and with the mysteries. This requires a certain amount of self-discipline and goodwill. If we have a tendency to forget to write thank-you letters or letters of acknowledgement, then we need the discipline and goodwill to remember and actually to write them. A relationship with the Solstices and Equinoxes requires similar careful attention. At one end of the spectrum we can simply notice the times of the year as they occur. At the other end of the spectrum we can focus our consciousness to honour the enormity of these outer and inner relationships, and take the opportunity of investigating these mysteries as a way deeper into God.

In Groups

The greatest solar celebrations with which we are familiar are those performed by the Druids at Stonehenge. In these rituals, disciplined disciples of the mysteries work carefully with the energies and symbolism of the Sun. In a temple meticulously constructed to reflect cosmic principles and channel cosmic energies, the Druid priests act as intermediaries between life on Earth and the life of the Solar Deity—invoking, channelling and blessing. In terms in no way intended to be crude, these festivals—particularly that of the Summer Solstice—have been described as solar orgasms fecundating the pranic energy field of Earth. Within these ceremonies, the Druids themselves ritually act out certain cosmic principles and the individual participants directly experience that which they have been studying.

This enactment by individuals of cosmic and mystic principles is a feature of all the great mystery rituals. In acting out a cosmic principle the ritualist draws down into herself the actual atmosphere and quality of that principle. What may have been only a distant meditative experience becomes an existential energetic reality. If one seeks that form of deep involvement within a traditional structure, then it makes sense to join an already existing ritual group.

If you are starting on your own or with a new group, then as always give any celebration some careful prior thought. My suggestion is that the individuals in a group sit down together several months in advance of the festival, meditate and share their inspirations. As I mentioned earlier, my sense is that there are no rules that need to be strictly adhered to and that our culture is in a position to create new forms, some completely original, others transformed syntheses of traditional ways that belong both to local indigenous cultures and cultures that are more distant.

If, however, there is one theme and motivation that will remain constant, it is the search for and revelation of inner meaning, which when externally celebrated will bring blessings for all life.

9
The Fire Festivals
Imbolc, Beltane,
Lammas & Samhain

The Four Fire Festivals

In the Celtic tradition of western Europe there are four Fire festivals which stand out as key celebrations during the year. They celebrate four distinct phases in the annual cycle of natural and horticultural fertility and growth: awakening, growth, harvest and rest. Some of these festivals are reflected in the sacred rhythms of other cultures around the globe and some have been appropriated by newer religions. Some cultures, of course, celebrate other aspects of the annual cycle. In describing the Fire festivals of the Celtic rhythm, therefore, I do not want to exclude other celebrations; nor do I want to suggest that this particular pattern be imposed on your own culture. The Celtic rhythm does, however, provide a basic matrix which can be a useful starting point.

These four Fire festivals are called Imbolc, Beltane, Lammas and Samhain. They are usually dated as follows, but these dates will, in fact, vary from locale to locale according to ecological conditions:

Imbolc—Awakening, February 1st.

Beltane—Growth, May 1st.

Lammas—Harvest, August 1st.

Samhain—Rest, October 31st

The Angelic and Devic Aspect

To understand the essence of the four Celtic Fire festivals we need to broaden our terms of reference. And as we understand their essence, we shall see that they are universal festivals and not restricted to the Celtic tradition.

But first I must confess a real problem for me in writing about their essence. The core feature of the Fire festivals is that they acknowledge and celebrate our relationship with the Earth and with the angelic and fairy realms; in particular these festivals honour the relationship between the seasons, nature and angelic cooperation. My problem is that I have no idea whether you, the reader, are sympathetic to the idea of an angelic and fairy reality, or whether you think this realm is purely mythical and with no foundation in real life.

It therefore seems appropriate to pause and examine devic reality for a few lines. Even if you do not or cannot accept that fairies and angels exist anywhere except in deluded imaginations, it is necessary to understand the delusion in order to understand the festivals.

First we need to appreciate that throughout history and in all cultures there have always been descriptions of other beings and creatures existing in a reality parallel to our own and interpenetrating with it. These beings occasionally pass through from their reality to ours, manifesting to human perception and then disappearing again. Academic anthropologists assume that the universality of these beings through all cultures is based in the fact that the structure of the human psyche and the elements of human existence are the same wherever we are. The theory is that we are insecure, surrounded by unknown forces which we personalise, giving them images and shapes drawn from our unconscious. According to the mainstream anthropologists, what we see as external and mysterious beings are simply the impersonal forces of nature. We have no control over them, but it is understandable that we should anthropomorphise them and pretend to be able to control them.

According to anthropologists with a more cosmic perspective, however, these phenomena are not impersonal forces, but are indeed real beings. In fact, there is a whole parallel world of these beings and it is not simply appropriate but crucial that we have a good relationship with this other dimension of life.

My own ongoing and unavoidable personal experience is of the reality of this parallel world, and I have made an attempt elsewhere to explain its purpose and dimension in a language that is logical and rational. The basic idea is that the world as we know it is divided into two intertwining dynamics. The first dynamic is that of atomic matter. This is the stuff we know all about. It is composed, at one level, of atoms and molecules, and they arrange themselves to create different life-forms. But examine the basic atom under a high-powered electron microscope, enter the world of quantum and sub-atomic physics, and we find not coherent bits of matter but electric particles which are also wave-forms and which are insubstantial.

Examined closely, there is nothing but wave energy. Examined less closely, there are the forms we can touch, see, smell and taste. The big question—for us and for modern science—is: what binds these wave forces into form? Science does not know. Esoteric philosophy suggests that it is an element as yet undiscovered by science. This element we call devic—as opposed to atomic—and it is the *bridging* dynamic which transforms sub-atomic waves and particles into tangible form. We thus have two basic building bricks in life: atomic particles and devic essence. (*Deva:* another Sanskrit word meaning 'shining, luminous being' and applied to all consciousnesses such as fairies, elves, cherubim, angels, archangels etc.)

Atomic matter, as we see it, arranges itself into a variety of life-forms which are distinguished by looking different, behaving differently and having different indwelling consciousnesses. The carbon in coal is the same carbon that is in plants, that is in animals, that is in human beings. But it is arranged in another way and the consciousness in the total structure is different. This is fantastic, isn't it? Precisely the same elements, but the form is as varied as a diamond, a rose, a tiger, a human being. Try to work out a way of explaining that to an alien.

Similarly, according to the esoteric traditions, devic essence also arranges itself in different ways and with different indwelling consciousnesses, to provide varying forms of devic existence: elementals, undines, salamanders, elves, gnomes, fairies, cherubim, seraphim, angels and archangels. All of these are substantially made up of devic essence. Equally, their major characteristic is coloured by being of devic essence. And the fundamental work of all devic beings is to help form and consciousness achieve their archetypal and divine potential. And the fundamental work of all devic beings is to help form and consciousness achieve their archetypal and divine potential.

Occult traditions through the ages have taught that there is this parallel life-stream which works with all manifest life. Unless you allow your poetic imagination freedom, unless you deliberately exercise the muscles of your occult sensitivity or unless you are naturally clairvoyant, all of this may sound so much rubbish. Once upon a time, there was no shame in talking of these realities, though we must recognise there was indeed manipulation of them in terms of fear and superstition. It is good that over the last few centuries superstition should have been exorcised from our culture, but it is a mistake to throw out the baby with the bath water. The superstition is exorcised—may it be gone forever—but the reality of the devic and angelic realms remains. There are many thousands of sane, grounded people who bear witness.

We do not see things as you do, in their solid, outer materialisations, but rather in their inner life-giving state. We deal with what is behind what you see or sense, but these are interconnected like different octaves of the same melody. What we see is different forms of life. (Dorothy

114

Maclean in *The Findhorn Garden*)

The fundamental idea is simple: Plants grow successfully and ecologies evolve successfully with the active cooperation of devas. In intimate relationship with the passing seasons—less light and cold, more light and warmth, and so on—the devas work, weaving patterns of growth and prana into plant life and the local ecology. The horticultural rhythm of preparation, planting, care, harvesting and rest are guided and influenced by a dancing relationship between local weather conditions, local devic influences and the day-to-day actions of horticulturists and farmers.

We have here a beautiful triangular relationship at the centre of which sits the plant and landscape itself:

Human Action

•

Plant/Landscape

•   •

Time/Ecology   Fairy/Angelic
Weather/Soil   Cooperation
Conditions

Candles, Flames and Fire

The Fire festivals, then, are a celebration of devic reality. For millennia, the most elementary way of honouring our relationship with the devic world has been to light a flame for it. Enter any sacred space, in any time period, on any part of the globe and we find sacred fire, a flame. Sit alone and light one candle. Watch and sense the change in atmosphere.

In a mystical way, in a perceptual way as the eye/brain plays with the dancing images of the flame, fire provides a bridge between our world and the devic world. You can achieve a similar perception with moving water and rising smoke, but neither have the dynamic and extraordinary quality of living fire. In elegant sacred ritual, within the confines of the holy sanctuary, candles are lit, the flames gracefully invoking angelic presence. In the Fire festivals—honouring the Earth, honouring procreation, abundance, fertility, the seasons and devic cooperation in all of this—*great* fires are lit. These great fires are signals to the local ecological community, inner and outer, of our thanks. We thank Gaia, we thank nature, we thank the plants and animals, and we thank all the beings of the devic realm who are so intimately involved with natural growth.

The Four Phases

Each of the Fire festivals, then, denotes a crucial moment in the ecological cycle. Each festival is a celebration of the triangular relationship between humanity, nature and the devic world. It is also an invocation for continued success and cooperation. These festivals honour Gaia and nature, they honour the power of fertile growth and they honour the angelic realm. This is no superstition, but a careful giving of attention to crucial relationships.

Imbolc is known as the first day of the Celtic Spring. Its keynote is that of *awakening*. It signals that the harshest times of Winter are past and a new surge of natural life-force is ready to thrust forth into growth. It is as if Mother Nature, deep in sleep, begins to move in her slumbers. The great angels of the landscape and the local ecology, through to the fairies and elves of individual plants, have also been sleeping, and now in their dream contemplation they become aware of the season that is to come.

This new surge of earthly life-force cannot begin yet, but there are signs, hints and feelings that it is stirring. It signals the moment when one can start preparing the earth for horticulture. The great fires of Imbolc are lit. Wake up! Win-

116

ter is not fully past, but Spring approaches. Prepare for the growth ahead. Finalise your plans. Know what you will plant. Prepare the seeds and bulbs. Begin to feel the earth. The great rhythm of cooperation—Earth, Sun, weather, angelic beings, human labour and the plants themselves —is about to begin.

Beltane is the second great fire. It celebrates the successful launch and process of the new year. In early May the major hard labour is complete. The ground has been prepared, the crops are planted and now the work is that of tending, guarding and caring. The fruits of labour are beginning to manifest.

The great fires of Beltane are now lit, calling for continued protection and cooperation, expressing gratitude for the cooperation that has been given and celebrating the richness of earthly life.

Lammas, at the beginning of August, is when the first real indications of the harvest can be seen. Indeed some harvesting begins and there is concern now for the safety and complete gathering of the crops. Again, it is a time for gratitude, but also for continued invocation and care. And the great fires of thanksgiving are lit once more.

Samhain then marks the end of the horticultural cycle. It takes place at the end of October and is also known as the Peace-Fire and the end of the Celtic year. Harvest is over. The ground has been prepared for Winter. The nature spirits, great and small, are returning to their cycle of inner contemplation. All activity has turned to peace and we prepare for the long nights ahead. It is now many weeks until the Winter Solstice and four Moons until Imbolc, Spring and the great rebirth.

Contemporary Celebration
In the distant past, each area had its wise women and men, its shamans, witches and wizards, its priests of nature. These men and women were attuned to the natural cycles

around them and knew the importance of harmony with nature, with the Earth and with the angelic realms. In the natural flow of their lives, they carefully observed the signs in their environment. They were like hunters who never stopped stalking nature. Following the pattern of time, observing the stars and the lunar rhythm, watching the signs of growth in the plant world, these careful, wise people would signal when the celebrations were due.

So what are we to do today with these great festivals? It is possible, as some groups do, to follow the ceremonies of tradition, to resurrect these ceremonies and transform them. But, as with all festivals, I believe that we need to begin in the privacy of our own hearts. We need first to make a relationship with the inner stimulus of the Fire festivals before we can work authentically with them. This means, again, that we are called to inner work.

In this case we are called to begin three distinct relationships. Our first is with Gaia and nature. Our second is with the plant and animal world and the landscape. And the third is with the angelic, fairy and devic world. These relationships also require the self-discipline of goodwill and attentiveness. They require that we walk upon this planet, within our environment, watching and stalking. Even in the cities, in the quiet of the night and at dawn, in the parks and among the trees on the pavements, in our own window boxes and houseplants, with our pets and other urban animals, we can stalk nature. We can watch the seasons change; we can feel them playing through our bodies. We can sense the devic life at work within the plant world. We can sense the soil of Gaia beneath the concrete, see clouds and blue sky above. We need to choose to be aware and to hold our focus.

Then in our celebrations we need to meditate our way into a sense of what these festivals and relationships most deeply signify to us and, having caught this sense, create our events. Our celebration may be as simple as the lighting of a candle or a walk to the nearest green space where we recite a poem to Pan. It may be a wonderful dance and party that swirls with the fertile energies of these times. It may be a great bonfire. It may be a private prayer.

Whatever the celebration, it will be a greeting and an honouring of crucial natural relationships, a small gesture of gratitude to the life and the lives which sustain us.

Afterword

What has surely become clear by now is that to celebrate these festivals and ceremonies is to enter into a natural book of wisdom. Year by year, festival by festival—as we study, meditate, enjoy and work with them—their inner meaning and dynamic become more clear. The festivals are incredible tools of learning. They ask us to see the sacred in all life and, more than that, they ask us to become actively involved in the sacred. Finally they seduce us into the recognition that we too are sacred.

Let them pass by with no acknowledgement and we live ignoring the sacred reality of our existence and of all existence.

New Rituals, Mailing List and Ceremonies Booklet
As you work with festivals and ceremonies, you may find certain approaches, rituals, prayers, invocations and dances which really work. Please send them to me at the Findhorn Press. I will be very interested to see them with the hope that in time to come they will be incorporated into a revised edition of this book. Equally, if you have a working interest in this area and would like to be on a mailing and networking list, please let me have your name and address.

If you are working with the three major ceremonies in this book, I suggest you photocopy the appropriate pages and then loose-bind them. In this way you can have the pages easily open as you work with them.

William Bloom,
Findhorn Press,
The Park,
Findhorn
Forres,
Scotland IV36 OTZ

Invocations

May the Sun in the head
And the Sun in the heart
Respond to the life emanating
From the Central Spiritual Sun
That the service of Love
May be rendered with perfection.

The Great Invocation

From the point of Light within the Mind of God
Let Light stream forth into the minds of men.
Let Light descend on Earth.

From the point of Love within the Heart of God
Let Love stream forth into the hearts of men.
May Christ return to Earth.

From the centre where the Will of God is known
Let purpose guide the little wills of men—
The purpose which the Masters know and serve.

From the centre which we call the race of men
Let the plan of Love and Light work out
And may it seal the door where evil dwells.

Let Light and Love and Power restore the Plan on Earth.

To All Beings

Love to All Beings
North—South—East—West
Above—Below
Love to All Beings

Compassion to All Beings
North—South—East—West
Above—Below
Compassion to All Beings

Joy to All Beings
North—South—East—West
Above—Below
Joy to All Beings

Peace to All Beings
North—South—East—West
Above—Below
Peace to All Beings

The Glastonbury Invocation

There is a source of Love which is the Heart of All Life
Let that Love flow
Source to Earth—Heart to Heart

There is a source of Light which is the Mind of All Life
Let that Light flow
Source to Earth—Mind to Mind

There is a source of Power which is the Purpose of All
Life
Let that Power flow
Source to Earth—Purpose to Purpose

We are that Love
We are that Light
We are that Power

Peace and Healing on Earth

Select Bibliography

Alice A. Bailey, *Discipleship in the New Age—Volumes 1 & 2*, Lucis Press, 1972.
—*Esoteric Astrology*, Lucis Press, 1951.
—*Externalisation of the Hierarchy*, Lucis Press, 1972.
William Bloom, *Meditation in a Changing World*, Gothic Image, 1987.
Janet and Colin Bord, *Earth Rites—Fertility Practices in Pre-Industrial England*, Granada, 1982.
Mordecai Brill, Marlene Halpin & William Genne (eds), *Write Your Own Wedding*, Association Press, 1973.
Jean Cooper, *The Aquarian Dictionary of Festivals*, Thorsons, 1990.
Howard Kirschenbaum & Rockwell Stensrud, *The Wedding Book—Alternative Ways to Celebrate Marriage*, Seabury, 1974.
Elisabeth Kübler-Ross, *On Death and Dying*, Macmillan New York, 1969.
Elisabeth Kübler-Ross, *Death: The Final Stage of Growth*, Prentice-Hall, 1975.
Stephen Levine, *Healing into Life and Death*, Anchor/Doubleday, 1987.
Kim Long, *The Moon Book*, Johnson Books, 1988.
Katie Marks, *Circle of Song: Chants, Dances and Ceremonies of Love, Healing and Power*. To be published Spring 1991 by Findhorn Press.
Benito Reyes, *Conscious Dying*, World University of America, Ojai, 1986.
Milo Shannon-Thornberry, *The Alternative Celebrations Catalogue*, Pilgrim Press, 1982.
Starhawk, *Dreaming the Dark*, Beacon Press, 1982.
—*The Spiral Dance: A Rebirth of the Ancient Religion of the Great Goddess*, Harper & Row, 1979.
Maria-Bagriel Wosien, *Sacred Dance*, Thames & Hudson, 1972.